The Champion's Faith - Wrestling and Achieving Spiritual Victory

Joshua Rhoades

Published by Joshua Paul Rhoades, 2024.

THE CHAMPION'S FAITH - WRESTLING AND ACHIEVING SPIRITUAL VICTORY

First edition. September 3, 2024.

ISBN: 979-8227649560

Written by Joshua Rhoades.

Also by Joshua Rhoades

Courage Under Fire: David's Stand On The Battlefield
Jonah's Journey: Voices Of Redemption And Lessons In Obedience
The Furnace Of Faith: 12 Principles From The Heat Of Faith
Whispers of Hope: Inspiring Stories of Men's Prayers In Scripture
Frontier Legends: The Oregon Dream
Elijah: A Beacon Of Boldness
HOOK, LINE & SAVIOUR - Faith Reflections from Fishing
Driven By Faith: Motor Racing Inspired Christian Life
30 Day Devotional - Bold and Strong- Coffee Devotions for a
Courageous Christian Walk
Authentic Christianity: The Heart of Old Time Religion
Consider The Ant - God's Tiny Preachers
Flee Fornication: The Plea For Purity
Renewed Hope- How to Find Encouragement in God
Sounding The Call - The Voice of Conviction
The Altar - Where Heaven Meets Earth
The Bible's Battlefields- Timeless Lessons from Ancient Wars
The Sacred Art of Silence - How Silence Speaks in Scripture
Under Fire- The Sanctity of the Traditional Biblical Home
Who Is on the Lord's Side? A Call to Righteousness
What Is Truth? - From Skepticism to Submission
First and Goal- Faith and Football Fundamentals
From Dugout to Devotion- Spiritual Lessons from Baseball
Par for the Course- Faith and Fairways
The Believer's Pace- Tools for Running Life's Marathon

The Immutable Fortress- Security in God's Unchanging Nature
Biblical Bravery
Deer Stands and Devotions: A Hunter's Walk with God
Jesus Knows- Our Hearts, Our Responsibility
Restoration - Setting The Bone
Spiritual 911- God's Word for Life's Emergency's
The Freedom of Forgiveness
The Jezebel Effect - Ancient Manipulations Modern Lessons
The Shout That Stopped The Saviour
The Time Machine Chronicles: Old Testament Characters
Anchored In Truth Exploring The Depths of Psalm 119
Biblical Counsel on Anger
Proverbs' Portraits The Men God Mentions
Stumbling in the Dark - The Dangers of Alcohol
The Champion's Faith - Wrestling and Achieving Spiritual Victory

Introduction
Chapter 1 Preparation
Chapter 2 Discipline
Chapter 3 Endurance
Chapter 4 Focus
Chapter 5 Strength
Chapter 6 Overcoming Opponents
Chapter 7 Training
Chapter 8 Perseverance
Chapter 9 Team Support
Chapter 10 Strategy
Chapter 11 Battling Temptation
Chapter 13 Humility
Chapter 14 Dedication
Chapter 15 Mental Toughness
Chapter 16 Consistency
Chapter 17 Focus on the Goal
Chapter 18 Overcoming Fear
Chapter 19 Integrity
Chapter 20 Learning from Defeat
Chapter 21 Courage
Chapter 22 Victory Celebration
Conclusion

Introduction

Wrestling is more than just a sport; it's a battle, a test of strength, strategy, and endurance. But what if the battles we face in life could be approached like a wrestling match? What if we could learn how to fight through challenges, not just in the ring, but in our everyday lives? "The Champion's Faith- Wrestling and Achieving Spiritual Victory" is about discovering how the principles of wrestling can help us grow in our faith and conquer the struggles we face. Just as wrestlers train hard to strengthen their bodies and sharpen their techniques, we need to train our hearts and minds to stand strong in our faith. This book will take you through the steps of building a champion's mindset, one that is focused on achieving victory through trust in God. You'll learn how to take on life's toughest opponents, like fear, doubt, and temptation, with the confidence that comes from knowing you're not alone in the fight. Each chapter will guide you through practical lessons and stories of wrestlers who overcame their battles by relying on their faith. Whether you're a wrestling fan or someone looking for spiritual encouragement, this book will show you how to wrestle with your challenges and emerge victorious with the strength and courage that only God can provide. Get ready to enter the ring and fight the good fight of faith, because with the right training, you can become a champion in both wrestling and life.

Chapter 1 Preparation

Preparation is an essential aspect of both wrestling and the Christian life, and it requires dedication, discipline, and a commitment to continuous improvement. In wrestling, athletes train rigorously to hone their skills, build their strength, and increase their endurance. This preparation involves a combination of physical training, mental conditioning, and strategic planning. Wrestlers spend countless hours in the gym, lifting weights, doing cardio workouts, and practicing wrestling techniques. They work on their agility, flexibility, and stamina, knowing that these attributes are crucial for success on the mat. Wrestling also requires a sharp mind, so wrestlers engage in mental conditioning to stay focused and handle the pressures of competition. They study their opponents, learn different wrestling styles, and develop strategies to counteract their opponents' moves. Nutrition is another vital part of a wrestler's preparation, as they need to maintain a healthy diet to keep their bodies in peak condition. All these elements come together to prepare a wrestler for the intense physical and mental demands of a match.

Similarly, Christians prepare for their spiritual journey through prayer, studying the Bible, and seeking God's guidance. This preparation is crucial for living a life that honors God and fulfills His purpose. Prayer is a way for Christians to communicate with God, seeking His wisdom, strength, and direction. It helps believers stay connected to God and align their hearts with His will. The Bible is a fundamental resource for Christians, providing guidance, encouragement, and instruction. Studying the Bible helps believers understand God's character, His promises, and His commands. It equips them with the knowledge they need to live righteously and make wise decisions. Memorizing scripture is also an important part of preparation, as it allows Christians to recall God's word in times of need and use it as a source of comfort and strength. Fellowship with other believers is another key aspect of preparation, as it provides support, accountability, and encouragement. By engaging in regular fellowship, Christians can grow in their faith, learn from others, and build strong, supportive relationships. Worship is also essential, as it helps Christians focus on God, express their gratitude, and strengthen their faith.

The verse 2 Timothy 2:15 emphasizes the importance of preparation: "Study to shew thyself approved unto God, a workman that needeth not to be ashamed, rightly dividing the word of truth." This verse highlights the need for diligence in studying God's word and applying it to one's life. It encourages believers to be thorough and dedicated in their spiritual preparation, ensuring that they are well-equipped to handle life's challenges and fulfill their divine calling. Just as wrestlers train rigorously to be ready for their matches, Christians must be diligent in their spiritual preparation to be effective in their walk with God.

Preparation in both wrestling and the Christian life involves setting goals and working diligently to achieve them. Wrestlers set specific goals for their training and competition, such as improving their strength, mastering new techniques, or winning matches. These goals provide motivation and direction, helping them stay focused and committed to their training regimen. Similarly, Christians set spiritual goals, such as growing in their faith, developing a deeper understanding of God's word, or serving others more effectively. These goals help believers stay focused on their spiritual journey and make intentional efforts to grow and improve.

Both wrestlers and Christians must also be prepared to face challenges and setbacks. In wrestling, athletes may experience injuries, losses, or periods of self-doubt. These challenges test their resolve and determination, but through preparation and perseverance, they can overcome them and emerge stronger. Similarly, Christians face spiritual battles, temptations, and trials that test their faith. By being well-prepared through prayer, Bible study, and fellowship, believers can navigate these challenges with confidence and resilience. James 1:2-4 encourages believers to view trials as opportunities for growth: "My brethren, count it all joy when ye fall into divers temptations; Knowing this, that the trying of your faith worketh patience. But let patience have her perfect work, that ye may be perfect and entire, wanting nothing."

Preparation also involves being adaptable and ready to adjust one's approach as needed. Wrestlers must be able to adapt their strategies based on their opponents' moves and the dynamics of the match. This flexibility allows them to respond effectively to unexpected situations and stay competitive. Similarly, Christians must be adaptable in their spiritual journey, being open to God's leading and willing to make changes as He directs. Proverbs 3:5-6 advises believers to trust in God's guidance: "Trust in the LORD with all thine heart; and lean not unto thine own understanding. In all thy ways acknowledge him, and he shall direct thy paths." By being adaptable and responsive to God's guidance, Christians can navigate their spiritual journey with wisdom and grace.

Both wrestlers and Christians benefit from the support and encouragement of others. Wrestlers often train with coaches, teammates, and mentors who provide guidance, feedback, and motivation. This support system helps them stay committed to their training and improve their performance. Similarly, Christians benefit from the support of their faith community, including pastors, mentors, and fellow believers. This community provides accountability, encouragement, and spiritual guidance, helping believers stay on track and grow in their faith. Hebrews 10:24-25 emphasizes the importance of fellowship: "And let us consider one another to provoke unto love and to good works: Not forsaking the assembling of ourselves together, as the manner of some is; but exhorting one another: and so much the more, as ye see the day approaching."

In both wrestling and the Christian life, preparation involves continuous learning and improvement. Wrestlers constantly seek to improve their skills, learn new techniques, and refine their strategies. They are always looking for ways to enhance their performance and gain an edge over their opponents. Similarly, Christians are called to continually grow in their faith, deepen their understanding of God's word, and become more Christ-like. This ongoing process of learning and growth helps believers become more effective in their spiritual journey and better equipped to serve others. 2 Peter 3:18 encourages believers to grow in their faith: "But grow in grace, and in the knowledge of our Lord and Saviour Jesus Christ. To him be glory both now and for ever. Amen."

Preparation also requires perseverance and dedication. Wrestlers must be committed to their training regimen, even when it is challenging or inconvenient. They must push through fatigue, discomfort, and setbacks to achieve their goals. Similarly, Christians must be dedicated to their spiritual disciplines, even when it is difficult. This perseverance helps believers stay focused on their spiritual journey and remain faithful to God's calling. Galatians 6:9 encourages perseverance: "And let us not be weary in well doing: for in due season we shall reap, if we faint not."

In conclusion, preparation is a critical aspect of both wrestling and the Christian life, requiring dedication, discipline, and a commitment to continuous improvement. Wrestlers train rigorously to hone their skills, build their strength, and increase their endurance, knowing that this preparation is essential for success on the mat. Similarly, Christians prepare for their spiritual journey through prayer, studying the Bible, and seeking God's guidance. This preparation equips believers with the tools they need to face life's challenges and fulfill their divine calling. The verse 2 Timothy 2:15 emphasizes the importance of diligent preparation, encouraging believers to be thorough and dedicated in their spiritual journey. By setting goals, being adaptable, seeking support, and persevering through challenges, both wrestlers and Christians can navigate their respective journeys with confidence and resilience. Through continuous learning and improvement, they can grow in their skills and faith, ultimately achieving their goals and fulfilling their purpose.

Chapter 2 Discipline

Discipline is crucial in both wrestling and the Christian life, as it involves maintaining strict practices, following routines, and making sacrifices to achieve goals. Wrestlers exhibit immense discipline in their training and diet, knowing that their performance on the mat depends on their dedication and self-control. They follow rigorous training schedules, often spending several hours a day in the gym or on the wrestling mat, honing their skills, improving their strength, and increasing their endurance. This training is not just physical but also mental, as wrestlers need to develop the focus and mental toughness required to compete at high levels. They engage in various exercises, drills, and sparring sessions to perfect their techniques and build muscle memory. Additionally, wrestlers must be disciplined in their diet, ensuring they eat the right foods in the right amounts to maintain their weight class and optimize their physical performance. This often means avoiding junk food, sticking to meal plans, and sometimes cutting weight in a healthy and controlled manner. The discipline required to maintain such a lifestyle is demanding, but it is essential for success in wrestling.

Similarly, Christians are called to practice spiritual disciplines to grow in their faith and live a life that honors God. Spiritual disciplines include practices such as prayer, Bible study, fasting, worship, and fellowship. These disciplines help believers draw closer to God, understand His will, and gain the strength and guidance needed to navigate life's challenges. Prayer is a fundamental discipline that allows Christians to communicate with God, seek His wisdom, and express their gratitude and concerns. Regular prayer helps believers stay connected to God and align their hearts with His purposes. Bible study is another critical discipline, as it provides believers with the knowledge and understanding of God's Word. By studying the Bible, Christians learn about God's character, His promises, and His commands, which guides their actions and decisions. Memorizing scripture is also a valuable discipline, as it allows believers to recall God's Word in times of need and use it as a source of encouragement and strength.

Fasting is a spiritual discipline that involves abstaining from food or other pleasures to focus on God and seek His guidance. It is a way to demonstrate dependence on God and cultivate self-control. Worship, both private and corporate, is another essential discipline that helps Christians express their love and reverence for God. Through worship, believers can experience God's presence, receive His comfort, and strengthen their faith. Fellowship with other believers is also crucial, as it provides support, accountability, and encouragement. By engaging in regular fellowship, Christians can grow in their faith, learn from others, and build strong, supportive relationships.

The verse 1 Corinthians 9:27 emphasizes the importance of discipline in the Christian life: "But I keep under my body, and bring it into subjection: lest that by any means, when I have preached to others, I myself should be a castaway." This verse highlights the need for self-control and discipline in order to live a life that is pleasing to God and effective in ministry. Just as wrestlers must be disciplined in their training and diet to compete successfully, Christians must be disciplined in their spiritual practices to grow in their faith and fulfill their calling.

Discipline in both wrestling and the Christian life involves setting goals and working diligently to achieve them. Wrestlers set specific goals for their training and competition, such as improving their strength, mastering new techniques, or winning matches. These goals provide motivation and direction, helping them stay focused and committed to their training regimen. Similarly, Christians set spiritual goals, such as growing in their faith, developing a deeper understanding of God's Word, or serving others more effectively. These goals help believers stay focused on their spiritual journey and make intentional efforts to grow and improve.

Both wrestlers and Christians must also be disciplined in overcoming challenges and setbacks. In wrestling, athletes may experience injuries, losses, or periods of self-doubt. These challenges test their resolve and determination, but through discipline and perseverance, they can overcome them and emerge stronger. Similarly, Christians face spiritual battles, temptations, and trials that test their faith. By maintaining discipline through prayer, Bible study, and fellowship, believers can navigate these challenges with confidence and resilience. James 1:2-4 encourages believers to view trials as opportunities for growth: "My brethren, count it all joy when ye fall into divers temptations; Knowing this, that the trying of your faith worketh patience. But let patience have her perfect work, that ye may be perfect and entire, wanting nothing."

Discipline also involves being consistent and committed to one's practices. Wrestlers must be consistent in their training, following their routines even when it is difficult or inconvenient. They must push through fatigue, discomfort, and setbacks to achieve their goals. Similarly, Christians must be consistent in their spiritual disciplines, dedicating time to prayer, Bible study, and worship even when it is challenging. This consistency helps believers stay focused on their spiritual journey and remain faithful to God's calling. Galatians 6:9 encourages perseverance and consistency: "And let us not be weary in well doing: for in due season we shall reap, if we faint not."

In both wrestling and the Christian life, discipline involves making sacrifices. Wrestlers often sacrifice their time, comfort, and sometimes even social activities to dedicate themselves to their training. They may miss out on certain foods or leisure activities to maintain their diet and fitness levels. These sacrifices are necessary to achieve their goals and perform at their best. Similarly, Christians are called to make sacrifices in their spiritual journey. This may involve giving up certain habits, comforts, or even relationships that hinder their walk with God. Romans 12:1 urges believers to offer their lives as a living sacrifice to God: "I beseech you therefore, brethren, by the mercies of God, that ye present your bodies a living sacrifice, holy, acceptable unto God, which is your reasonable service." These sacrifices help Christians grow in their faith and live a life that is pleasing to God.

Support and accountability are also crucial aspects of discipline in both wrestling and the Christian life. Wrestlers often train with coaches, teammates, and mentors who provide guidance, feedback, and motivation. This support system helps them stay committed to their training and improve their performance. Similarly, Christians benefit from the support of their faith community, including pastors, mentors, and fellow believers. This community provides accountability, encouragement, and spiritual guidance, helping believers stay on track and grow in their faith. Hebrews 10:24-25 emphasizes the importance of fellowship and accountability: "And let us consider one another to provoke unto love and to good works: Not forsaking the assembling of ourselves together, as the manner of some is; but exhorting one another: and so much the more, as ye see the day approaching."

Discipline also involves learning from mistakes and failures. Wrestlers may lose matches or make errors during competitions, but these experiences provide valuable lessons that help them improve. They analyze their performances, identify areas for improvement, and work diligently to correct their mistakes. This process of learning and growth is essential for success in wrestling. Similarly, Christians may experience failures or setbacks in their spiritual journey, but these experiences can lead to growth and maturity. By reflecting on their mistakes, seeking God's forgiveness, and making necessary changes, believers can grow stronger in their faith. Proverbs 24:16 reminds us that even when we fall, we can rise again: "For a just man falleth seven times, and riseth up again: but the wicked shall fall into mischief."

In both wrestling and the Christian life, discipline is a lifelong journey. Wrestlers continually strive to improve their skills, stay in shape, and compete at higher levels. This ongoing process requires dedication, perseverance, and a commitment to continuous improvement. Similarly, Christians are called to continually grow in their faith, deepen their understanding of God's Word, and become more Christ-like. This lifelong journey of discipline and growth helps believers become more effective in their spiritual journey and better equipped to serve others. 2 Peter 3:18 encourages believers to grow in grace and knowledge: "But grow in grace, and in the knowledge of our Lord and Saviour Jesus Christ. To him be glory both now and for ever. Amen."

In conclusion, discipline is a critical aspect of both wrestling and the Christian life, requiring dedication, self-control, and a commitment to continuous improvement. Wrestlers maintain strict discipline in their training and diet to compete successfully, knowing that this discipline is essential for their performance. Similarly, Christians practice spiritual disciplines such as prayer, Bible study, fasting, worship, and fellowship to grow in their faith and live a life that honors God. The verse 1 Corinthians 9:27 emphasizes the importance of discipline, encouraging believers to keep their bodies and minds under control to avoid being disqualified in their spiritual journey. By setting goals, making sacrifices, seeking support, and learning from mistakes, both wrestlers and Christians can navigate their respective journeys with confidence and resilience. Through consistent discipline and a commitment to growth, they can achieve their goals and fulfill their purpose, ultimately bringing glory to God and experiencing the rewards of their dedication and perseveranc

Chapter 3 Endurance

Endurance is an essential quality in both wrestling and the Christian life, demanding perseverance, resilience, and the ability to push through challenges and hardships. In wrestling, athletes must endure grueling matches that test their physical and mental limits. These matches can be intense and exhausting, requiring wrestlers to maintain their strength, agility, and focus even when they are fatigued and in pain. Wrestlers train rigorously to build their endurance, engaging in various exercises that enhance their cardiovascular fitness, muscular strength, and mental toughness. They run, lift weights, and practice wrestling techniques repeatedly to prepare their bodies and minds for the demands of competition. This rigorous training helps wrestlers develop the stamina needed to perform at their best throughout the match, even when faced with challenging opponents and adverse conditions. Endurance in wrestling is not just about physical stamina; it also involves mental resilience. Wrestlers must stay focused, maintain a positive mindset, and keep pushing forward even when they are tired or facing setbacks. They learn to manage their energy, pace themselves, and use strategic thinking to outlast their opponents. The ability to endure through difficult matches and remain determined is what often separates successful wrestlers from those who fall short.

Similarly, Christians are called to endure trials and tribulations in their spiritual journey. The Christian life is often marked by challenges, temptations, and hardships that test believers' faith and perseverance. Endurance in the Christian context involves remaining faithful to God, trusting in His promises, and continuing to follow His guidance even when faced with difficulties. James 1:12 emphasizes the importance of endurance in the Christian life: "Blessed is the man that endureth temptation: for when he is tried, he shall receive the crown of life, which the Lord hath promised to them that love him." This verse highlights the reward for enduring through trials – the crown of life promised by God to those who love Him. Enduring through life's challenges requires spiritual strength and resilience, much like the endurance needed in wrestling.

Prayer is a key aspect of building endurance in the Christian life. Through prayer, believers can seek God's strength, guidance, and comfort during difficult times. Prayer helps Christians stay connected to God, allowing them to draw on His power and remain steadfast in their faith. It provides a way to express their struggles, seek wisdom, and find solace in God's presence. Regular prayer strengthens believers' spiritual endurance, enabling them to face life's challenges with confidence and trust in God's plan.

Bible study is another important discipline that helps Christians build endurance. By studying God's Word, believers can gain insight into His character, His promises, and His instructions for living a faithful life. The Bible provides encouragement and hope, reminding Christians of God's faithfulness and the eternal rewards awaiting those who endure. Scriptures like Romans 5:3-4 encourage believers to view trials as opportunities for growth: "And not only so, but we glory in tribulations also: knowing that tribulation worketh patience; And patience, experience; and experience, hope." By immersing themselves in God's Word, Christians can develop the spiritual strength and resilience needed to endure through trials.

Fellowship with other believers is also crucial for building endurance. The support, encouragement, and accountability provided by a faith community can help Christians stay strong and persevere through difficult times. Sharing struggles, praying for one another, and offering words of encouragement can bolster believers' resolve and help them remain faithful. Hebrews 10:24-25 emphasizes the importance of fellowship: "And let us consider one another to provoke unto love and to good works: Not forsaking the assembling of ourselves together, as the manner of some is; but exhorting one another: and so much the more, as ye see the day approaching." By staying connected to a supportive community, Christians can draw strength from one another and endure through life's challenges.

Just as wrestlers must endure through intense physical exertion, Christians must endure through spiritual battles. Wrestling matches can be physically draining, with athletes pushing their bodies to the limit to secure a victory. Similarly, Christians face spiritual battles that require them to resist temptation, overcome doubts, and remain faithful in the face of adversity. Ephesians 6:12 reminds believers of the spiritual nature of these battles: "For we wrestle not against flesh and blood, but against principalities, against powers, against the rulers of the darkness of this world, against spiritual wickedness in high places." By relying on God's strength and putting on the full armor of God, Christians can stand firm and endure through these spiritual battles.

Endurance in both wrestling and the Christian life also involves learning from setbacks and failures. Wrestlers may lose matches or face injuries, but these experiences can serve as valuable learning opportunities. By analyzing their performances, identifying areas for improvement, and making necessary adjustments, wrestlers can grow stronger and more resilient. Similarly, Christians may experience failures or setbacks in their spiritual journey, but these experiences can lead to growth and maturity. By reflecting on their mistakes, seeking God's forgiveness, and learning from their experiences, believers can develop greater spiritual endurance. Proverbs 24:16 offers encouragement: "For a just man falleth seven times, and riseth up again: but the wicked shall fall into mischief." This verse reminds Christians that even when they fall, they can rise again and continue their journey with renewed strength.

Both wrestlers and Christians benefit from setting goals and maintaining a clear focus on their objectives. Wrestlers set goals for their training, competitions, and overall performance, which provide motivation and direction. These goals help them stay committed to their training regimen and push through challenges. Similarly,

Christians set spiritual goals, such as growing in their faith, deepening their understanding of God's Word, or serving others more effectively. These goals help believers stay focused on their spiritual journey and remain motivated to endure through trials. Philippians 3:14 encourages believers to press toward their spiritual goals: "I press toward the mark for the prize of the high calling of God in Christ Jesus."

In both wrestling and the Christian life, endurance is developed through consistent practice and perseverance. Wrestlers train regularly, following disciplined routines to build their strength and stamina. They push through fatigue, discomfort, and setbacks, knowing that consistent effort is key to achieving their goals. Similarly, Christians develop spiritual endurance through consistent practice of spiritual disciplines, such as prayer, Bible study, and worship. By persevering in these practices, even when it is difficult, believers can strengthen their faith and build the resilience needed to endure through life's challenges. Galatians 6:9 encourages perseverance: "And let us not be weary in well doing: for in due season we shall reap, if we faint not."

Support and encouragement from others play a vital role in building endurance. Wrestlers often train with coaches, teammates, and mentors who provide guidance, feedback, and motivation. This support system helps them stay committed to their training and improve their performance. Similarly, Christians benefit from the support of their faith community, including pastors, mentors, and fellow believers. This community provides accountability, encouragement, and spiritual guidance, helping believers stay strong and persevere through difficult times. Ecclesiastes 4:9-10 highlights the importance of mutual support: "Two are better than one; because they have a good reward for their labour. For if they fall, the one will lift up his fellow: but woe to him that is alone when he falleth; for he hath not another to help him up."

In both wrestling and the Christian life, endurance involves a deep sense of purpose and determination. Wrestlers compete with the goal of achieving victory, improving their skills, and reaching their full potential. This sense of purpose drives them to endure through the challenges and sacrifices required in their sport. Similarly, Christians endure through trials with the ultimate goal of eternal life with God. This eternal perspective provides believers with hope and motivation to persevere through difficulties. Romans 8:18 offers encouragement: "For I reckon that the sufferings of this present time are not worthy to be compared with the glory which shall be revealed in us." By keeping their eyes on the ultimate reward, Christians can find the strength to endure through life's trials.

Both wrestlers and Christians must also practice self-discipline to maintain their endurance. Wrestlers follow strict training and diet regimens, making sacrifices to stay in peak physical condition. They resist temptations that could undermine their performance, such as unhealthy foods or skipping workouts. Similarly, Christians practice self-discipline in their spiritual lives, dedicating time to prayer, Bible study, and worship, and resisting temptations that could lead them astray. 1 Corinthians 9:25-27 emphasizes the importance of self-discipline: "And every man that striveth for the mastery is temperate in all things. Now they do it to obtain a corruptible crown; but we an incorruptible. I therefore so run, not as uncertainly; so fight I, not as one that beateth the air: But I keep under my body, and bring it into subjection: lest that by any means, when I have preached to others, I myself should be a castaway." By practicing self-discipline, believers can build the endurance needed to stay faithful and committed to their spiritual journey.

Endurance in both wrestling and the Christian life also involves a willingness to embrace challenges and push beyond one's comfort zone. Wrestlers constantly push themselves to improve, taking on tougher opponents and more challenging training regimens. They understand that growth and improvement come from facing and overcoming difficult challenges. Similarly, Christians are called to embrace the challenges and trials they face, viewing them as opportunities for growth and spiritual refinement. James 1:2-4 encourages believers to embrace trials with joy: "My brethren, count it all joy when ye fall into divers temptations; Knowing this, that the trying of your faith worketh patience. But let patience have her perfect work, that ye may be perfect and entire, wanting nothing." By embracing challenges and pushing beyond their comfort zones, Christians can develop greater endurance and become more like Christ.

Chapter 4 Focus

Focus is incredibly important in both wrestling and the Christian life, requiring individuals to maintain concentration, clarity, and dedication to their goals. In wrestling, staying focused during matches is crucial for success. Wrestlers must be acutely aware of their own movements, their opponent's tactics, and the dynamics of the match. They have to concentrate on executing their techniques with precision while constantly adapting to the ever-changing conditions on the mat. A single lapse in focus can result in a mistake that could cost them the match. To stay focused, wrestlers engage in rigorous training and mental conditioning. They practice visualization techniques to mentally prepare for matches, run through scenarios in their minds, and develop strategies to handle different situations. This mental preparation helps them stay calm and focused under pressure, allowing them to perform at their best when it matters most.

Similarly, Christians are called to focus on their spiritual journey, keeping their eyes on Jesus and remaining steadfast in their faith. The verse Hebrews 12:2 highlights the importance of focus in the Christian life: "Looking unto Jesus the author and finisher of our faith; who for the joy that was set before him endured the cross, despising the shame, and is set down at the right hand of the throne of God." This verse encourages believers to fix their gaze on Jesus, who is the ultimate example of faith and endurance. By focusing on Jesus, Christians can navigate the challenges of life with confidence and perseverance, knowing that He is guiding them every step of the way.

In both wrestling and the Christian life, maintaining focus requires discipline and commitment. Wrestlers must train consistently, follow strict routines, and avoid distractions that could hinder their performance. They need to stay disciplined in their diet, sleep, and overall lifestyle to ensure they are in peak physical and mental condition. This level of discipline helps them maintain the focus needed to perform well in matches. Similarly, Christians must practice spiritual disciplines such as prayer, Bible study, and worship to stay focused on their relationship with God. These practices help believers keep their hearts and minds aligned with God's will, enabling them to stay focused on their spiritual journey. Regular prayer allows Christians to communicate with God, seek His guidance, and strengthen their connection with Him. Studying the Bible provides insight into God's character, His promises, and His instructions for living a faithful life. Worship helps believers express their love and reverence for God, deepening their relationship with Him.

Focus also involves setting clear goals and working diligently to achieve them. Wrestlers set specific goals for their training and competition, such as improving their techniques, building strength, or winning matches. These goals provide motivation and direction, helping them stay focused and committed to their training regimen. Similarly, Christians set spiritual goals, such as growing in their faith, developing a deeper understanding of God's Word, or serving others more effectively. These goals help believers stay focused on their spiritual journey and make intentional efforts to grow and improve. Philippians 3:14 encourages believers to press toward their spiritual goals: "I press toward the mark for the prize of the high calling of God in Christ Jesus."

Both wrestlers and Christians must also be prepared to face distractions and challenges that can divert their focus from their goals. In wrestling, distractions can come in many forms, such as the noise of the crowd, the pressure of competition, or the actions of their opponent. Wrestlers must learn to tune out these distractions and remain focused on their strategy and performance. Similarly, Christians face distractions in their daily lives that can shift their focus away from their spiritual goals. These distractions can include materialism, social pressures, and personal struggles. By staying rooted in their faith and continually seeking God's guidance, believers can overcome these distractions and keep their eyes on Jesus.

Perseverance is another essential quality for maintaining focus. Wrestlers face numerous challenges, such as injuries, losses, and periods of self-doubt. Despite these obstacles, they must persevere, staying determined and resilient to reach their goals. This perseverance is fueled by their passion for the sport, their commitment to their team, and their desire to achieve their goals. Similarly, Christians are called to persevere in their faith, even when faced with trials and temptations. James 1:12 encourages believers to persevere: "Blessed is the man that endureth temptation: for when he is tried, he shall receive the crown of life, which the Lord hath promised to them that love him." By persevering through difficulties, Christians grow stronger in their faith and develop a deeper reliance on God.

Support and encouragement from others are crucial for maintaining focus. Wrestlers rely on their coaches, teammates, and supporters to help them stay focused and motivated. Coaches provide guidance, feedback, and strategic advice, while teammates offer encouragement and camaraderie. This support network helps wrestlers stay committed to their training and focused on their goals. Similarly, Christians rely on the support and encouragement of their fellow believers. The Christian community provides a network of support through prayer, accountability, and mutual encouragement. Hebrews 10:24-25 highlights the importance of this support: "And let us consider one another to provoke unto love and to good works: Not forsaking the assembling of ourselves together, as the manner of some is; but exhorting one another: and so much the more, as ye see the day approaching." By supporting and encouraging each other, Christians can help one another stay focused on their spiritual goals.

Adaptability is also essential for maintaining focus. In wrestling, conditions can change rapidly, requiring wrestlers to adjust their strategies and make quick decisions. Whether it's a sudden change in their opponent's tactics, an unexpected move, or an injury, wrestlers must be ready to adapt and find the best way forward. Similarly, Christians must be adaptable in their spiritual journey, ready to adjust their plans and approaches as they seek God's guidance. Proverbs 3:5-6 encourages believers to trust in God's direction: "Trust in the LORD with all thine heart; and lean not unto thine own understanding. In all thy ways acknowledge him, and he shall direct thy paths." By being flexible and open to God's leading, Christians can navigate their spiritual race more effectively.

Both wrestlers and Christians must also set their sights on the ultimate goal, keeping their eyes on the prize. In wrestling, the goal is to win the match and achieve victory. This goal drives wrestlers to push their limits, stay focused, and persevere through challenges. Similarly, Christians run their race with the ultimate goal of eternal life with God. Philippians 3:13-14 captures this forward-looking determination: "Brethren, I count not myself to have apprehended: but this one thing I do, forgetting those things which are behind, and reaching forth unto those things which are before, I press toward the mark for the prize of the high calling of God in Christ Jesus." By keeping their eyes on the ultimate prize, Christians can stay motivated and committed to their faith journey.

Resilience is another important quality for maintaining focus. Wrestlers often face setbacks, such as losses, injuries, and periods of self-doubt. Their resilience drives them to recover quickly, learn from their experiences, and get back on the mat. This resilience is a key component of their success. Similarly, Christians encounter setbacks and failures in their spiritual journey, but resilience helps them rise again, seek God's forgiveness, and continue striving to follow Christ. Proverbs 24:16 highlights this resilience: "For a just man falleth seven times, and riseth up again: but the wicked shall fall into mischief." By maintaining a resilient spirit, believers can overcome obstacles and grow stronger in their faith.

Both wrestlers and Christians must also practice self-discipline to maintain their focus on their goals. In wrestling, self-discipline involves following strict training regimens, maintaining a healthy diet, and avoiding distractions. This discipline helps wrestlers stay focused and perform at their best. Similarly, Christians must practice self-discipline in their spiritual lives, dedicating time to prayer, Bible study, and worship. This discipline helps believers stay focused on their faith journey and grow in their relationship with God. 1 Corinthians 9:25-27 illustrates the importance of discipline: "And every man that striveth for the mastery is temperate in all things. Now they do it to obtain a corruptible crown; but we an incorruptible. I therefore so run, not as uncertainly; so fight I, not as one that beateth the air: But I keep under my body, and bring it into subjection: lest that by any means, when I have preached to others, I myself should be a castaway."

In both wrestling and the Christian life, maintaining focus involves a sense of order and stability. In wrestling, the rules ensure that matches are conducted fairly and safely, providing a structured environment for competition. This orderliness helps prevent chaos and confusion, allowing wrestlers to focus on their performance. Similarly, God's commandments provide a sense of order and stability in the lives of believers. By following God's instructions, Christians can navigate the complexities of life with confidence, knowing that they are guided by divine wisdom. Proverbs 3:5-6 encourages believers to trust in God's guidance: "Trust in the LORD with all thine heart; and lean not unto thine own understanding. In all thy ways acknowledge him, and he shall direct thy paths." By trusting in God's commandments, Christians can experience the peace and stability that come from living in alignment with His will.

In both wrestling and the Christian life, focus helps build a sense of community and shared values. Wrestlers, their teams, and fans are united by their commitment to the sport's principles and values. This shared commitment fosters a sense of camaraderie, respect, and mutual support among participants and spectators. Similarly, God's commandments create a sense of community among believers, who are united by their shared faith and commitment to living according to God's Word. This unity is expressed through worship, fellowship, and acts of service, as believers come together to support and encourage one another. Hebrews 10:24-25 highlights the importance of this sense of community: "And let us consider one another to provoke unto love and to good works: Not forsaking the assembling of ourselves together, as the manner of some is; but exhorting one another: and so much the more, as ye see the day approaching." By building a strong sense of community and shared values, Christians can create an environment that fosters spiritual growth and mutual support.

In conclusion, focus is a crucial element in both wrestling and the Christian life, requiring individuals to maintain concentration, clarity, and dedication to their goals. In wrestling, athletes must stay focused during matches, concentrating on their movements, their opponent's tactics, and the dynamics of the match. This focus is developed through rigorous training, mental conditioning, and disciplined lifestyle choices. Similarly, Christians are called to focus on their spiritual journey, keeping their eyes on Jesus and remaining steadfast in their faith. The verse Hebrews 12:2 encourages believers to fix their gaze on Jesus, who is the ultimate example of faith and endurance. By practicing spiritual disciplines, setting clear goals, and persevering through challenges, Christians can maintain their focus and grow in their relationship with God. Support from others, adaptability, resilience, self-discipline, and a sense of order and community further strengthen this focus. By maintaining a clear and unwavering focus on their goals, both wrestlers and Christians can achieve their objectives and fulfill their purpose, ultimately bringing glory to God and experiencing the rewards of their dedication and perseverance.

Chapter 5 Strength

Strength is crucial in both wrestling and the Christian life, though it manifests differently in each context. Wrestlers rely on physical strength to perform well in matches, using their muscles and endurance to overpower their opponents and execute complex maneuvers. Physical strength in wrestling is developed through rigorous training routines that include weightlifting, cardiovascular exercises, and practicing wrestling techniques. Wrestlers spend countless hours in the gym building their muscles, increasing their stamina, and enhancing their agility. They follow strict diets to ensure their bodies are in peak condition, consuming the right balance of proteins, carbohydrates, and fats to fuel their workouts and aid in muscle recovery. This physical preparation is essential because wrestling matches are intense and physically demanding. Wrestlers must lift, throw, and pin their opponents, all of which require significant strength. Moreover, physical strength helps wrestlers maintain control during a match, resist their opponents' attacks, and endure the grueling demands of the sport.

In contrast, Christians rely on spiritual strength to navigate their faith journey and overcome life's challenges. Spiritual strength is the inner power that comes from a deep relationship with God and the empowerment of the Holy Spirit. This strength is cultivated through prayer, reading and meditating on the Bible, worship, and fellowship with other believers. Philippians 4:13 highlights the source of this strength: "I can do all things through Christ which strengtheneth me." This verse reminds Christians that their ability to face difficulties and accomplish their goals comes from Christ, who provides them with the necessary strength and support. Just as wrestlers train their bodies to become strong, Christians engage in spiritual practices to build their inner strength. Prayer is a vital aspect of this training, as it allows believers to communicate with God, seek His guidance, and receive His comfort. Through prayer, Christians can find peace and reassurance, knowing that God is with them and will help them through any situation.

Reading and meditating on the Bible is another important way Christians build their spiritual strength. The Bible is filled with stories of God's faithfulness, promises, and instructions for living a godly life. By immersing themselves in Scripture, Christians can draw strength from God's Word, gaining wisdom and encouragement for their daily lives. Verses like Isaiah 40:31 offer hope and reassurance: "But they that wait upon the LORD shall renew their strength; they shall mount up with wings as eagles; they shall run, and not be weary; and they shall walk, and not faint." This verse emphasizes the idea that those who trust in God will receive renewed strength to face their challenges.

Worship is another practice that strengthens Christians spiritually. Through worship, believers express their love and gratitude to God, lifting their hearts and voices in praise. Worship can take many forms, including singing, praying, and reflecting on God's goodness. It helps Christians focus on God, reminding them of His greatness and power. Worship also brings believers into God's presence, where they can experience His peace and strength. Fellowship with other believers is equally important for building spiritual strength. The Christian community provides support, encouragement, and accountability, helping individuals grow in their faith. By sharing their struggles, praying for one another, and offering words of encouragement, believers can strengthen each other and build a sense of unity. Hebrews 10:24-25 highlights the importance of fellowship: "And let us consider one another to provoke unto love and to good works: Not forsaking the assembling of ourselves together, as the manner of some is; but exhorting one another: and so much the more, as ye see the day approaching."

Both wrestlers and Christians must also learn to rely on their respective sources of strength during times of difficulty. In wrestling, athletes face numerous challenges, such as injuries, tough opponents, and the physical demands of training and competition. They must rely on their physical strength to push through these obstacles, stay focused, and continue striving for success. Similarly, Christians face trials, temptations, and hardships that test their faith and resilience. In these moments, they must rely on their spiritual strength, trusting in God to provide the power and endurance they need to persevere. James 1:12 encourages believers to remain steadfast: "Blessed is the man that endureth temptation: for when he is tried, he shall receive the crown of life, which the Lord hath promised to them that love him."

Building strength, whether physical or spiritual, requires consistency and dedication. Wrestlers must train regularly, following a disciplined regimen to maintain and improve their strength. This consistency helps them stay in peak condition and perform at their best during matches. Similarly, Christians must consistently engage in spiritual practices to maintain and grow their spiritual strength. Daily prayer, Bible study, worship, and fellowship are essential for staying connected to God and drawing on His strength. Galatians 6:9 emphasizes the importance of perseverance: "And let us not be weary in well doing: for in due season we shall reap, if we faint not."

Another parallel between wrestling and the Christian life is the importance of rest and recovery. Wrestlers understand that rest is a crucial component of their training regimen. Proper rest allows their muscles to recover and grow stronger, preventing injuries and ensuring they are ready for the next challenge. Similarly, Christians need periods of rest and spiritual renewal to maintain their strength. Jesus Himself took time to rest and pray, setting an example for His followers. Matthew 11:28-30 offers an invitation to rest: "Come unto me, all ye that labour and are heavy laden, and I will give you rest. Take my yoke upon you, and learn of me; for I am meek and lowly in heart: and ye shall find rest unto your souls. For my yoke is easy, and my burden is light." By taking time to rest in God's presence, Christians can renew their spiritual strength and find peace.

Support from others plays a vital role in building and maintaining strength. Wrestlers often have coaches, teammates, and trainers who provide guidance, encouragement, and assistance. This support system helps them stay motivated, improve their skills, and overcome challenges. Similarly, Christians benefit from the support of their faith community, including pastors, mentors, and fellow believers. This community provides spiritual guidance, encouragement, and accountability, helping individuals grow in their faith and stay strong. Ecclesiastes 4:9-10 highlights the value of mutual support: "Two are better than one; because they have a good reward for their labour. For if they fall, the one will lift up his fellow: but woe to him that is alone when he falleth; for he hath not another to help him up."

Both wrestlers and Christians must also practice self-discipline to build and maintain their strength. Wrestlers follow strict training schedules and dietary plans, making sacrifices to stay in peak physical condition. They resist temptations that could undermine their performance, such as unhealthy foods or skipping workouts. Similarly, Christians practice self-discipline in their spiritual lives, dedicating time to prayer, Bible study, and worship, and resisting temptations that could lead them away from God. 1 Corinthians 9:25-27 illustrates the importance of discipline: "And every man that striveth for the mastery is temperate in all things. Now they do it to obtain a corruptible crown; but we an incorruptible. I therefore so run, not as uncertainly; so fight I, not as one that beateth the air: But I keep under my body, and bring it into subjection: lest that by any means, when I have preached to others, I myself should be a castaway."

In both wrestling and the Christian life, strength is not just about individual effort but also about reliance on a higher power. Wrestlers rely on their training, coaches, and support system to build and maintain their strength. They understand that their success is not solely dependent on their efforts but also on the guidance and support they receive. Similarly, Christians rely on God for their strength, recognizing that true spiritual strength comes from Him. Philippians 4:13 reminds believers of this truth: "I can do all things through Christ which strengtheneth me." By relying on God, Christians can find the strength to face any challenge and accomplish their goals.

Both wrestlers and Christians must also be adaptable and resilient, using their strength to overcome obstacles and adjust to changing circumstances. In wrestling, matches can be unpredictable, and athletes must be able to adapt their strategies and use their strength effectively in different situations. Similarly, Christians face various trials and challenges in their spiritual journey and must rely on their spiritual strength to navigate these difficulties. Romans 8:28 offers reassurance: "And we know that all things work together for good to them that love God, to them who are the called according to his purpose." By trusting in God's plan and using their spiritual strength, Christians can overcome obstacles and grow in their faith.

Both contexts emphasize the importance of perseverance and determination in building and maintaining strength. Wrestlers must persevere through tough training sessions, injuries, and losses, staying committed to their goals and continuing to push themselves. This perseverance helps them build greater strength and resilience. Similarly, Christians must persevere in their faith, remaining steadfast in their spiritual practices and trusting in God's promises even when faced with trials. James 1:2-4 encourages believers to embrace perseverance: "My brethren, count it all joy when ye fall into divers temptations; Knowing this, that the trying of your faith worketh patience. But let patience have her perfect work, that ye may be perfect and entire, wanting nothing."

In conclusion, strength is a critical aspect of both wrestling and the Christian life, though it manifests differently in each context. Wrestlers rely on physical strength, developed through rigorous training, disciplined diets, and consistent practice. This physical strength enables them to perform well in matches, maintain control, and endure the demands of the sport. Similarly, Christians rely on spiritual strength, cultivated through prayer, Bible study, worship, and fellowship. This spiritual strength empowers them to navigate life's challenges, remain faithful, and fulfill their God-given purpose. Philippians 4:13 highlights the source of this strength: "I can do all things through Christ which strengtheneth me." By relying on Christ, Christians can find the strength to face any challenge and achieve their goals. Both wrestlers and Christians must also practice self-discipline, rely on support from others, and persevere through difficulties to build and maintain their strength. Through consistent effort, dedication, and reliance on a higher power, individuals in both contexts can develop the strength needed to succeed and fulfill their purpose.

Chapter 6 Overcoming Opponents

In both wrestling and the Christian life, overcoming opponents is a central theme that requires strategy, strength, and determination. Wrestlers face physical opponents in the ring, engaging in intense matches where they must use their strength, skill, and mental toughness to prevail. Each match is a test of their abilities, as they grapple with their opponent, attempting to pin them or gain points through effective moves and holds. Wrestlers train rigorously to develop the techniques and strength needed to overpower their opponents. They practice various maneuvers, such as takedowns, throws, and pins, to outsmart and outmuscle their competitors. The preparation for these matches involves hours of practice, studying their opponents' strengths and weaknesses, and developing strategies to counteract their opponents' moves. Wrestlers must stay focused and adaptable, ready to respond to their opponents' actions and capitalize on any opportunities to gain an advantage. Overcoming opponents in wrestling requires a combination of physical prowess, strategic thinking, and mental resilience.

Similarly, Christians face spiritual battles that require overcoming various opponents. These opponents are not physical but spiritual, including temptations, doubts, fears, and the influences of a world that often stands in opposition to God's ways. Ephesians 6:12 explains the nature of these battles: "For we wrestle not against flesh and blood, but against principalities, against powers, against the rulers of the darkness of this world, against spiritual wickedness in high places." This verse highlights that Christians are engaged in a spiritual struggle against powerful forces that seek to undermine their faith and lead them away from God. To overcome these spiritual opponents, Christians must rely on their faith, the strength provided by God, and the spiritual armor described in Ephesians 6:13-18. This armor includes the belt of truth, the breastplate of righteousness, the gospel of peace, the shield of faith, the helmet of salvation, and the sword of the Spirit, which is the Word of God. By putting on this armor, Christians are equipped to stand firm against the attacks of the enemy and overcome the challenges they face.

In both wrestling and the Christian life, overcoming opponents requires perseverance and determination. Wrestlers must endure the physical demands of their sport, pushing through fatigue, pain, and the mental strain of competition. They must stay focused on their goals, continually pushing themselves to improve and overcome the obstacles they encounter in each match. Similarly, Christians must persevere in their faith, remaining steadfast in their commitment to God even when faced with trials and temptations. James 1:12 encourages believers to persevere: "Blessed is the man that endureth temptation: for when he is tried, he shall receive the crown of life, which the Lord hath promised to them that love him." By enduring through difficult times and staying faithful to God, Christians can overcome their spiritual opponents and receive the rewards promised by God.

Both wrestlers and Christians benefit from having a strong support system to help them overcome their opponents. Wrestlers often have coaches, teammates, and mentors who provide guidance, encouragement, and support. These individuals help wrestlers refine their techniques, develop effective strategies, and stay motivated throughout their training and competitions. Similarly, Christians benefit from the support of their faith community, including pastors, mentors, and fellow believers. This community provides spiritual guidance, encouragement, and accountability, helping individuals grow in their faith and stay strong in the face of spiritual battles. Hebrews 10:24-25 emphasizes the importance of mutual support: "And let us consider one another to provoke unto love and to good works: Not forsaking the assembling of ourselves together, as the manner of some is; but exhorting one another: and so much the more, as ye see the day approaching." By supporting one another, believers can help each other overcome spiritual opponents and remain steadfast in their faith.

In both contexts, preparation is key to overcoming opponents. Wrestlers prepare for their matches through rigorous training, studying their opponents, and developing strategies to gain an advantage. This preparation helps them build the physical strength, skill, and mental toughness needed to succeed in the ring. Similarly, Christians prepare for spiritual battles through prayer, studying the Bible, and growing in their relationship with God. Prayer helps believers stay connected to God, seek His guidance, and draw on His strength. Studying the Bible provides Christians with the knowledge and wisdom needed to understand God's will and apply it to their lives. By immersing themselves in God's Word, believers can learn how to resist temptation, overcome doubt, and stand firm in their faith. Psalm 119:11 highlights the importance of knowing God's Word: "Thy word have I hid in mine heart, that I might not sin against thee." By preparing through prayer and Bible study, Christians can build the spiritual strength and resilience needed to overcome their spiritual opponents.

Both wrestlers and Christians must also be adaptable and ready to adjust their strategies as needed. In wrestling, matches can be unpredictable, and athletes must be able to adapt their tactics based on their opponents' actions and the flow of the match. This adaptability allows wrestlers to respond effectively to challenges and seize opportunities to gain an advantage. Similarly, Christians must be adaptable in their spiritual journey, ready to adjust their plans and approaches as they seek God's guidance and face various challenges. Proverbs 3:5-6 encourages believers to trust in God's direction: "Trust in the LORD with all thine heart; and lean not unto thine own understanding. In all thy ways acknowledge him, and he shall direct thy paths." By being flexible and open to God's leading, Christians can navigate their spiritual battles more effectively and overcome their opponents.

Resilience is another important quality for overcoming opponents in both wrestling and the Christian life. Wrestlers often face setbacks, such as losses, injuries, and periods of self-doubt. Their resilience drives them to recover quickly, learn from their experiences, and get back on the mat. This resilience is a key component of their success. Similarly, Christians encounter setbacks and failures in their spiritual journey, but resilience helps them rise again, seek God's forgiveness, and continue striving to follow Christ. Proverbs 24:16 highlights this resilience: "For a just man falleth seven times, and riseth up again: but the wicked shall fall into mischief." By maintaining a resilient spirit, believers can overcome obstacles and grow stronger in their faith.

In both wrestling and the Christian life, overcoming opponents also involves relying on a higher power. Wrestlers rely on their training, coaches, and support system to help them succeed in their matches. They understand that their success is not solely dependent on their efforts but also on the guidance and support they receive. Similarly, Christians rely on God for their strength, recognizing that true spiritual victory comes from Him. Philippians 4:13 reminds believers of this truth: "I can do all things through Christ which strengtheneth me." By relying on God, Christians can find the strength to face any challenge and overcome their spiritual opponents.

Both wrestlers and Christians must also practice self-discipline to overcome their opponents. Wrestlers follow strict training schedules and dietary plans, making sacrifices to stay in peak physical condition. They resist temptations that could undermine their performance, such as unhealthy foods or skipping workouts. Similarly, Christians practice self-discipline in their spiritual lives, dedicating time to prayer, Bible study, and worship, and resisting temptations that could lead them away from God. 1 Corinthians 9:25-27 illustrates the importance of discipline: "And every man that striveth for the mastery is temperate in all things. Now they do it to obtain a corruptible crown; but we an incorruptible. I therefore so run, not as uncertainly; so fight I, not as one that beateth the air: But I keep under my body, and bring it into subjection: lest that by any means, when I have preached to others,

I myself should be a castaway." By practicing self-discipline, believers can build the strength and focus needed to overcome their spiritual opponents.

In both wrestling and the Christian life, overcoming opponents involves a deep sense of purpose and determination. Wrestlers compete with the goal of achieving victory, improving their skills, and reaching their full potential. This sense of purpose drives them to endure the challenges and sacrifices required in their sport. Similarly, Christians overcome spiritual opponents with the ultimate goal of eternal life with God. This eternal perspective provides believers with hope and motivation to persevere through difficulties. Romans 8:18 offers encouragement: "For I reckon that the sufferings of this present time are not worthy to be compared with the glory which shall be revealed in us." By keeping their eyes on the ultimate reward, Christians can find the strength to overcome their spiritual battles.

In conclusion, overcoming opponents is a central theme in both wrestling and the Christian life, requiring strategy, strength, and determination. Wrestlers face physical opponents in the ring, using their skills and strength to prevail in intense matches. They train rigorously, study their opponents, and develop strategies to gain an advantage. Similarly, Christians face spiritual battles against powerful forces that seek to undermine their faith. Ephesians 6:12 explains the nature of these battles: "For we wrestle not against flesh and blood, but against principalities, against powers, against the rulers of the darkness of this world, against spiritual wickedness in high places." To overcome these spiritual opponents, Christians rely on their faith, the strength provided by God, and the spiritual armor described in Ephesians 6:13-18. Both wrestlers and Christians benefit from strong support systems, preparation, adaptability, resilience, and self-discipline. By maintaining a deep sense of purpose and relying on a higher power, individuals in both contexts can overcome their opponents and achieve their goals, ultimately bringing glory to God and experiencing the rewards of their perseverance and dedication.

Chapter 7 Training

Training is a fundamental aspect of both wrestling and the Christian life, requiring dedication, consistency, and a commitment to growth. Wrestlers train regularly to develop their physical strength, endurance, and technical skills. They follow rigorous training routines that include weightlifting, cardio exercises, and practicing wrestling techniques. This consistent training helps them build muscle, improve their stamina, and perfect their moves, ensuring they are in peak condition for their matches. Wrestlers spend countless hours in the gym and on the mat, working tirelessly to enhance their performance. They also focus on their diet, eating nutritious foods to fuel their bodies and maintain their weight class. Training in wrestling is not just about physical preparation; it also involves mental conditioning. Wrestlers practice visualization techniques to prepare mentally for their matches, strategizing and imagining different scenarios they might face. This mental training helps them stay focused, calm, and confident under pressure. The discipline required for regular training in wrestling helps athletes develop resilience, perseverance, and a strong work ethic.

Similarly, Christians are called to train in godliness, cultivating spiritual disciplines that help them grow in their faith and live a life that honors God. 1 Timothy 4:8 highlights the value of spiritual training: "For bodily exercise profiteth little: but godliness is profitable unto all things, having promise of the life that now is, and of that which is to come." This verse emphasizes that while physical exercise has some value, training in godliness is far more beneficial, impacting both the present life and eternity. Spiritual training involves practices such as prayer, reading and meditating on the Bible, worship, and fellowship with other believers. Through these disciplines, Christians can deepen their relationship with God, gain wisdom and understanding, and receive the strength and guidance needed to navigate life's challenges.

Prayer is a vital component of spiritual training, allowing Christians to communicate with God, seek His guidance, and express their gratitude and concerns. Regular prayer helps believers stay connected to God and align their hearts with His will. It provides a source of comfort, strength, and encouragement, especially during difficult times. Through prayer, Christians can find peace and reassurance, knowing that God is with them and will help them through any situation. Studying the Bible is another crucial aspect of training in godliness. The Bible is the inspired Word of God, providing instruction, encouragement, and insight into His character and will. By reading and meditating on Scripture, Christians can learn more about God's promises, His commandments, and His plan for their lives. This knowledge equips them to live righteously, make wise decisions, and resist temptation. Memorizing Scripture is also beneficial, as it allows believers to recall God's Word in times of need and use it as a source of strength and encouragement. Psalm 119:11 highlights the importance of knowing God's Word: "Thy word have I hid in mine heart, that I might not sin against thee."

Worship is another important practice in spiritual training. Through worship, Christians express their love and reverence for God, lifting their hearts and voices in praise. Worship can take many forms, including singing, praying, and reflecting on God's goodness. It helps believers focus on God, reminding them of His greatness and power. Worship also brings believers into God's presence, where they can experience His peace and strength. Fellowship with other believers is equally important for training in godliness. The Christian community provides support, encouragement, and accountability, helping individuals grow in their faith. By engaging in regular fellowship, Christians can learn from others, share their struggles and victories, and build strong, supportive relationships. Hebrews 10:24-25 emphasizes the importance of fellowship: "And let us consider one another to provoke unto love and to good works: Not forsaking the assembling of ourselves together, as the manner of some is; but exhorting one another: and so much the more, as ye see the day approaching."

Both wrestlers and Christians must be disciplined and consistent in their training. Wrestlers follow strict training schedules and dietary plans, making sacrifices to stay in peak physical condition. They push through fatigue, discomfort, and setbacks, knowing that consistent effort is key to achieving their goals. Similarly, Christians must consistently engage in spiritual disciplines to grow in their faith and stay strong in their walk with God. Daily prayer, Bible study, worship, and fellowship are essential for staying connected to God and drawing on His strength. Galatians 6:9 encourages perseverance: "And let us not be weary in well doing: for in due season we shall reap, if we faint not."

Both wrestlers and Christians benefit from having a strong support system to help them stay committed to their training. Wrestlers often have coaches, teammates, and trainers who provide guidance, encouragement, and assistance. This support system helps them stay motivated, improve their skills, and overcome challenges. Similarly, Christians benefit from the support of their faith community, including pastors, mentors, and fellow believers. This community provides spiritual guidance, encouragement, and accountability, helping individuals grow in their faith and stay strong. Ecclesiastes 4:9-10 highlights the value of mutual support: "Two are better than one; because they have a good reward for their labour. For if they fall, the one will lift up his fellow: but woe to him that is alone when he falleth; for he hath not another to help him up."

Both wrestlers and Christians must also be adaptable and ready to adjust their training as needed. In wrestling, athletes must be able to adapt their training routines based on their progress, injuries, and the demands of upcoming matches. This adaptability allows them to respond effectively to challenges and continue improving. Similarly, Christians must be adaptable in their spiritual journey, ready to adjust their practices and approaches as they seek God's guidance and face various challenges. Proverbs 3:5-6 encourages believers to trust in God's direction: "Trust in the LORD with all thine heart; and lean not unto thine own understanding. In all thy ways acknowledge him, and he shall direct thy paths." By being flexible and open to God's leading, Christians can navigate their spiritual journey more effectively and grow in their faith.

Training in both wrestling and the Christian life involves setting clear goals and working diligently to achieve them. Wrestlers set specific goals for their training and competition, such as improving their techniques, building strength, or winning matches. These goals provide motivation and direction, helping them stay focused and committed to their training regimen. Similarly, Christians set spiritual goals, such as growing in their faith, developing a deeper understanding of God's Word, or serving others more effectively. These goals help believers stay focused on their spiritual journey and make intentional efforts to grow and improve. Philippians 3:14 encourages believers to press toward their spiritual goals: "I press toward the mark for the prize of the high calling of God in Christ Jesus."

Both wrestlers and Christians must also learn to rely on their respective sources of strength during times of difficulty. Wrestlers face numerous challenges, such as injuries, tough opponents, and the physical demands of training and competition. They must rely on their physical strength, mental toughness, and the support of their coaches and teammates to push through these obstacles. Similarly, Christians face trials, temptations, and hardships that test their faith and resilience. In these moments, they must rely on their spiritual strength, trusting in God to provide the power and endurance they need to persevere. Philippians 4:13 reminds believers of this source of strength: "I can do all things through Christ which strengtheneth me." By relying on God, Christians can find the strength to face any challenge and continue growing in their faith.

Rest and recovery are also important aspects of training in both wrestling and the Christian life. Wrestlers understand that rest is crucial for muscle recovery, preventing injuries, and maintaining overall health. Proper rest allows their bodies to heal and grow stronger, ensuring they are ready for the next challenge. Similarly, Christians need periods of rest and spiritual renewal to maintain their strength and grow in their faith. Jesus Himself took time to rest and pray, setting an example for His followers. Matthew 11:28-30 offers an invitation to rest: "Come unto me, all ye that labour and are heavy laden, and I will give you rest. Take my yoke upon you, and learn of me; for I am meek and lowly in heart: and ye shall find rest unto your souls. For my yoke is easy, and my burden is light." By taking time to rest in God's presence, Christians can renew their spiritual strength and find peace.

In both wrestling and the Christian life, training requires resilience and perseverance. Wrestlers often face setbacks, such as losses, injuries, and periods of self-doubt. Their resilience drives them to recover quickly, learn from their experiences, and get back on the mat. This resilience is a key component of their success. Similarly, Christians encounter setbacks and failures in their spiritual journey, but resilience helps them rise again, seek God's forgiveness, and continue striving to follow Christ. Proverbs 24:16 highlights this resilience: "For a just man falleth seven times, and riseth up again: but the wicked shall fall into mischief." By maintaining a resilient spirit, believers can overcome obstacles and grow stronger in their faith.

Both wrestlers and Christians must also practice self-discipline to stay committed to their training. Wrestlers follow strict training schedules and dietary plans, making sacrifices to stay in peak physical condition. They resist temptations that could undermine their performance, such as unhealthy foods or skipping workouts. Similarly, Christians practice self-discipline in their spiritual lives, dedicating time to prayer, Bible study, and worship, and resisting temptations that could lead them away from God. 1 Corinthians 9:25-27 illustrates the importance of discipline: "And every man that striveth for the mastery is temperate in all things. Now they do it to obtain a corruptible crown; but we an incorruptible. I therefore so run, not as uncertainly; so fight I, not as one that beateth the air: But I keep under

my body, and bring it into subjection: lest that by any means, when I have preached to others, I myself should be a castaway." By practicing self-discipline, believers can build the strength and focus needed to grow in their faith and live a life that honors God.

In conclusion, training is a fundamental aspect of both wrestling and the Christian life, requiring dedication, consistency, and a commitment to growth. Wrestlers train regularly to develop their physical strength, endurance, and technical skills, following rigorous routines and making sacrifices to stay in peak condition. Similarly, Christians are called to train in godliness, cultivating spiritual disciplines such as prayer, Bible study, worship, and fellowship. 1 Timothy 4:8 highlights the value of spiritual training: "For bodily exercise profiteth little: but godliness is profitable unto all things, having promise of the life that now is, and of that which is to come." By consistently engaging in these practices, Christians can deepen their relationship with God, gain wisdom and understanding, and receive the strength and guidance needed to navigate life's challenges. Both wrestlers and Christians benefit from strong support systems, adaptability, resilience, self-discipline, and setting clear goals. By staying committed to their training and relying on their respective sources of strength, individuals in both contexts can achieve their goals, grow in their abilities, and fulfill their purpose.

Chapter 8 Perseverance

Perseverance is crucial in both wrestling and the Christian life, requiring individuals to endure pain, overcome obstacles, and remain steadfast in their commitment to their goals. In wrestling, athletes must persevere through intense physical pain and mental challenges to succeed. Wrestlers engage in rigorous training routines that push their bodies to the limit, including weightlifting, cardiovascular exercises, and practicing wrestling techniques. These training sessions can be grueling, causing muscle soreness, fatigue, and even injuries. Despite these challenges, wrestlers must persevere, knowing that consistent effort and determination are essential for improving their skills and achieving success in matches. They learn to push through the pain, stay focused on their goals, and maintain a positive mindset even when faced with setbacks. Wrestling matches themselves are tests of perseverance, as athletes must endure the physical demands of grappling with an opponent, the mental strain of strategizing and adapting to their opponent's moves, and the pressure of performing under the watchful eyes of coaches, teammates, and spectators. Wrestlers often face situations where they feel exhausted and overwhelmed, but their perseverance drives them to keep fighting, to keep pushing their limits, and to give their best effort until the very end.

Similarly, Christians are called to persevere in their faith, remaining steadfast in their commitment to God despite the trials and tribulations they face. The Christian life is often marked by challenges, including temptations, doubts, and hardships that test believers' faith and resolve. Perseverance in the Christian context involves trusting in God's promises, maintaining faith in His goodness, and continuing to follow His guidance even when circumstances are difficult. Romans 5:3-4 emphasizes the value of perseverance: "And not only so, but we glory in tribulations also: knowing that tribulation worketh patience; And patience, experience; and experience, hope." This verse highlights that tribulations are opportunities for growth, developing patience and character, and ultimately leading to hope. Christians are encouraged to view their trials as part of God's refining process, shaping them into stronger, more faithful individuals.

Prayer is a key aspect of building perseverance in the Christian life. Through prayer, believers can seek God's strength, guidance, and comfort during difficult times. Regular prayer helps Christians stay connected to God, allowing them to draw on His power and remain steadfast in their faith. It provides a way to express their struggles, seek wisdom, and find solace in God's presence. Studying the Bible is another important practice that helps Christians build perseverance. By immersing themselves in God's Word, believers can gain insight into His character, His promises, and His instructions for living a faithful life. The Bible provides encouragement and hope, reminding Christians of God's faithfulness and the eternal rewards awaiting those who persevere. Scriptures like James 1:12 offer encouragement: "Blessed is the man that endureth temptation: for when he is tried, he shall receive the crown of life, which the Lord hath promised to them that love him." By meditating on such verses, Christians can strengthen their resolve and find the courage to persevere through their trials.

Worship is another practice that helps Christians persevere. Through worship, believers express their love and reverence for God, lifting their hearts and voices in praise. Worship can take many forms, including singing, praying, and reflecting on God's goodness. It helps Christians focus on God, reminding them of His greatness and power. Worship also brings believers into God's presence, where they can experience His peace and strength. Fellowship with other believers is equally important for building perseverance. The Christian community provides support, encouragement, and accountability, helping individuals grow in their faith. By sharing their struggles, praying for one another, and offering words of encouragement, believers can strengthen each other and build a sense of unity. Hebrews 10:24-25 emphasizes the importance of fellowship: "And let us consider one another to provoke unto love and to good works: Not forsaking the assembling of ourselves together, as the manner of some is; but exhorting one another: and so much the more, as ye see the day approaching."

Both wrestlers and Christians must also be disciplined and consistent in their efforts to persevere. Wrestlers follow strict training schedules and dietary plans, making sacrifices to stay in peak physical condition. They push through fatigue, discomfort, and setbacks, knowing that consistent effort is key to achieving their goals. Similarly, Christians must consistently engage in spiritual disciplines to grow in their faith and stay strong in their walk with God. Daily prayer, Bible study, worship, and fellowship are essential for staying connected to God and drawing on His strength. Galatians 6:9 encourages perseverance: "And let us not be weary in well doing: for in due season we shall reap, if we faint not."

Both wrestlers and Christians benefit from having a strong support system to help them persevere. Wrestlers often have coaches, teammates, and trainers who provide guidance, encouragement, and assistance. This support system helps them stay motivated, improve their skills, and overcome challenges. Similarly, Christians benefit from the support of their faith community, including pastors, mentors, and fellow believers. This community provides spiritual guidance, encouragement, and accountability, helping individuals grow in their faith and stay strong. Ecclesiastes 4:9-10 highlights the value of mutual support: "Two are better than one; because they have a good reward for their labour. For if they fall, the one will lift up his fellow: but woe to him that is alone when he falleth; for he hath not another to help him up."

Both wrestlers and Christians must also be adaptable and ready to adjust their approaches as needed. In wrestling, matches can be unpredictable, and athletes must be able to adapt their strategies based on their opponents' actions and the flow of the match. This adaptability allows wrestlers to respond effectively to challenges and seize opportunities to gain an advantage. Similarly, Christians must be adaptable in their spiritual journey, ready to adjust their plans and approaches as they seek God's guidance and face various challenges. Proverbs 3:5-6 encourages believers to trust in God's direction: "Trust in the LORD with all thine heart; and lean not unto thine own understanding. In all thy ways acknowledge him, and he shall direct thy paths." By being flexible and open to God's leading, Christians can navigate their spiritual race more effectively.

Resilience is another important quality for persevering in both wrestling and the Christian life. Wrestlers often face setbacks, such as losses, injuries, and periods of self-doubt. Their resilience drives them to recover quickly, learn from their experiences, and get back on the mat. This resilience is a key component of their success. Similarly, Christians encounter setbacks and failures in their spiritual journey, but resilience helps them rise again, seek God's forgiveness, and continue striving to follow Christ. Proverbs 24:16 highlights this resilience: "For a just man falleth seven times, and riseth up again: but the wicked shall fall into mischief." By maintaining a resilient spirit, believers can overcome obstacles and grow stronger in their faith.

Both wrestlers and Christians must also practice self-discipline to persevere. Wrestlers follow strict training schedules and dietary plans, making sacrifices to stay in peak physical condition. They resist temptations that could undermine their performance, such as unhealthy foods or skipping workouts. Similarly, Christians practice self-discipline in their spiritual lives, dedicating time to prayer, Bible study, and worship, and resisting temptations that could lead them away from God. 1 Corinthians 9:25-27 illustrates the importance of discipline: "And every man that striveth for the mastery is temperate in all things. Now they do it to obtain a corruptible crown; but we an incorruptible. I therefore so run, not as uncertainly; so fight I, not as one that beateth the air: But I keep under my body, and bring it into subjection: lest that by any means, when I have preached to others, I myself should be a castaway." By practicing self-discipline, believers can build the strength and focus needed to persevere in their faith.

In both wrestling and the Christian life, perseverance involves a deep sense of purpose and determination. Wrestlers compete with the goal of achieving victory, improving their skills, and reaching their full potential. This sense of purpose drives them to endure the challenges and sacrifices required in their sport. Similarly, Christians persevere with the ultimate goal of eternal life with God. This eternal perspective provides believers with hope and motivation to endure through difficulties. Romans 8:18 offers encouragement: "For I reckon that the sufferings of this present time are not worthy to be compared with the glory which shall be revealed in us." By keeping their eyes on the ultimate reward, Christians can find the strength to persevere through their trials.

Both wrestlers and Christians must also learn to rely on their respective sources of strength during times of difficulty. Wrestlers face numerous challenges, such as injuries, tough opponents, and the physical demands of training and competition. They must rely on their physical strength, mental toughness, and the support of their coaches and teammates to push through these obstacles. Similarly, Christians face trials, temptations, and hardships that test their faith and resilience. In these moments, they must rely on their spiritual strength, trusting in God to provide the power and endurance they need to persevere. Philippians 4:13 reminds believers of this source of strength: "I can do all things through Christ which strengtheneth me." By relying on God, Christians can find the strength to face any challenge and continue growing in their faith.

Rest and recovery are also important aspects of perseverance in both wrestling and the Christian life. Wrestlers understand that rest is crucial for muscle recovery, preventing injuries, and maintaining overall health. Proper rest allows their bodies to heal and grow stronger, ensuring they are ready for the next challenge. Similarly, Christians need periods of rest and spiritual renewal to maintain their strength and grow in their faith. Jesus Himself took time to rest and pray, setting an example for His followers. Matthew 11

:28-30 offers an invitation to rest: "Come unto me, all ye that labour and are heavy laden, and I will give you rest. Take my yoke upon you, and learn of me; for I am meek and lowly in heart: and ye shall find rest unto your souls. For my yoke is easy, and my burden is light." By taking time to rest in God's presence, Christians can renew their spiritual strength and find peace.

In both wrestling and the Christian life, perseverance requires resilience and determination. Wrestlers often face setbacks, such as losses, injuries, and periods of self-doubt. Their resilience drives them to recover quickly, learn from their experiences, and get back on the mat. This resilience is a key component of their success. Similarly, Christians encounter setbacks and failures in their spiritual journey, but resilience helps them rise again, seek God's forgiveness, and continue striving to follow Christ. Proverbs 24:16 highlights this resilience: "For a just man falleth seven times, and riseth up again: but the wicked shall fall into mischief." By maintaining a resilient spirit, believers can overcome obstacles and grow stronger in their faith.

In conclusion, perseverance is a crucial element in both wrestling and the Christian life, requiring individuals to endure pain, overcome obstacles, and remain steadfast in their commitment to their goals. Wrestlers persevere through intense physical pain and mental challenges, pushing their bodies to the limit through rigorous training routines and enduring the physical demands of wrestling matches. Similarly, Christians are called to persevere in their faith, remaining steadfast in their commitment to God despite the trials and tribulations they face. Romans 5:3-4 emphasizes the value of perseverance: "And not only so, but we glory in tribulations also: knowing that tribulation worketh patience; And patience, experience; and experience, hope." By engaging in practices such as prayer, Bible study, worship, and fellowship, Christians can build the spiritual strength and resilience needed to persevere through life's challenges. Both wrestlers and Christians benefit from strong support systems, adaptability, resilience, self-discipline, and a deep sense of purpose. By staying committed to their goals and relying on their respective sources of strength, individuals in both contexts can overcome obstacles, achieve their goals, and fulfill their purpose, ultimately bringing glory to God and experiencing the rewards of their perseverance and dedication.

Chapter 9 Team Support

Team support is crucial in both wrestling and the Christian life, providing encouragement, guidance, and a sense of community that helps individuals thrive. In wrestling, athletes often have coaches and teammates who play significant roles in their development and success. Coaches provide essential guidance, teaching wrestlers techniques, strategies, and skills needed to excel in the sport. They offer feedback, helping wrestlers correct mistakes and improve their performance. Coaches also serve as motivators, encouraging wrestlers to push through challenges and stay focused on their goals. They help wrestlers develop mental toughness, instilling confidence and resilience that are crucial during competitions. Teammates, on the other hand, offer camaraderie and support. They train together, share experiences, and motivate each other. This sense of belonging to a team creates a supportive environment where wrestlers can grow and succeed. Teammates celebrate each other's victories and provide comfort and encouragement during setbacks. The bonds formed within a wrestling team can be strong and lasting, providing a network of support that extends beyond the mat.

Similarly, Christians are called to support one another, fostering a sense of community and mutual encouragement that strengthens their faith. Hebrews 10:24-25 emphasizes the importance of this support:

"And let us consider one another to provoke unto love and to good works: Not forsaking the assembling of ourselves together, as the manner of some is; but exhorting one another: and so much the more, as ye see the day approaching." This verse highlights the need for believers to gather together, encourage each other, and spur one another on toward love and good deeds. In the Christian life, support comes in many forms, including prayer, fellowship, and acts of service. Believers pray for one another, lifting each other's needs to God and seeking His intervention and blessings. This prayer support can be incredibly powerful, providing comfort and strength during difficult times.

Fellowship is another vital aspect of team support in the Christian life. By regularly gathering with other believers, Christians can share their experiences, learn from one another, and build strong, supportive relationships. Fellowship provides a sense of belonging and community, reminding believers that they are not alone in their faith journey. It offers opportunities for mutual encouragement, accountability, and growth. Through fellowship, Christians can challenge each other to grow in their faith, support each other through trials, and celebrate together in times of joy. Acts of service also play a crucial role in supporting one another in the Christian community. Believers are called to serve each other, meeting practical needs and demonstrating Christ's love through their actions. This service can take many forms, such as providing meals for those in need, helping with household tasks, offering a listening ear, or providing financial assistance. By serving one another, Christians can build a strong, caring community where everyone feels valued and supported.

Both wrestlers and Christians benefit from having mentors and role models who provide guidance and inspiration. In wrestling, coaches and experienced teammates often serve as mentors, sharing their knowledge and experience to help younger or less experienced wrestlers improve. These mentors offer valuable insights, advice, and encouragement, helping wrestlers navigate the challenges of the sport and reach their full potential. Similarly, in the Christian life, mentors and spiritual leaders play a crucial role in guiding believers in their faith journey. Pastors, elders, and more mature Christians can offer wisdom, support, and encouragement, helping others grow in their understanding of God's Word and deepen their relationship with Him. Mentorship provides accountability and support, ensuring that believers stay on the right path and continue to grow in their faith.

Both wrestlers and Christians must also be willing to offer support to others, recognizing that being part of a team or community involves giving as well as receiving. Wrestlers can support their teammates by offering encouragement, sharing tips and techniques, and being there for each other during difficult times. This mutual support strengthens the team and helps each member reach their potential. Similarly, Christians are called to support one another by praying for each other, offering words of encouragement, and serving one another in love. Galatians 6:2 encourages believers to "bear ye one another's burdens, and so fulfil the law of Christ." By supporting each other, Christians can create a strong, caring community where everyone feels valued and uplifted.

Both contexts emphasize the importance of unity and working together toward a common goal. In wrestling, team success depends on the collective efforts of all members, with each person contributing their skills and support to help the team achieve its objectives. This sense of unity fosters a positive, collaborative environment where everyone works together to succeed. Similarly, in the Christian life, believers are called to work together to advance God's kingdom and fulfill His purposes. Ephesians 4:16 illustrates this unity: "From whom the whole body fitly joined together and compacted by that which every joint supplieth, according to the effectual working in the measure of every part, maketh increase of the body unto the edifying of itself in love." By working together and supporting one another, Christians can achieve greater things for God's glory and build a strong, unified community.

Both wrestlers and Christians must also be adaptable and open to receiving support in different forms. In wrestling, support can come from various sources, including coaches, teammates, family, and friends. Being open to this support and willing to accept help when needed can make a significant difference in an athlete's success. Similarly, Christians should be open to receiving support from their faith community, recognizing that God often works through others to provide encouragement, guidance, and assistance. This openness to support helps believers stay connected to their community and strengthens their faith.

Both wrestlers and Christians benefit from regular gatherings that provide opportunities for support and encouragement. Wrestlers often attend team practices, competitions, and meetings where they can train together, share experiences, and support each other. These gatherings help build team cohesion and foster a sense of unity and mutual support. Similarly, Christians are encouraged to regularly gather for worship, Bible study, prayer meetings, and fellowship events. These gatherings provide opportunities for believers to connect with one another, share their faith journey, and receive encouragement and support. Regular attendance at these gatherings helps Christians stay connected to their faith community and strengthens their relationship with God.

Both wrestlers and Christians must also be willing to invest time and effort into building strong relationships within their community. In wrestling, building strong bonds with coaches and teammates requires time, effort, and a willingness to be vulnerable and open with one another. These relationships provide a foundation of trust and support that can help wrestlers navigate the challenges of the sport and achieve their goals. Similarly, Christians must invest time and effort into building strong relationships within their faith community. This involves being open and honest with one another, sharing experiences, and actively participating in community activities. Building these relationships creates a supportive environment where believers can grow in their faith and receive the encouragement and support they need.

Both wrestlers and Christians must also recognize the importance of giving back to their community. In wrestling, experienced athletes can give back by mentoring younger teammates, sharing their knowledge and experience, and helping to build a strong team culture. This not only benefits the younger wrestlers but also strengthens the team as a whole. Similarly, Christians are called to give back to their faith community by using their gifts and talents to serve others. 1 Peter 4:10 encourages believers to use their gifts to serve one another: "As every man hath received the gift, even so minister the same one to another, as good stewards of the manifold grace of God." By giving back, Christians can help build a strong, vibrant community that reflects God's love and serves His purposes.

In conclusion, team support is a crucial element in both wrestling and the Christian life, providing encouragement, guidance, and a sense of community that helps individuals thrive. Wrestlers often have coaches and teammates who play significant roles in their development and success, offering guidance, feedback, and motivation. Similarly, Christians are called to support one another, fostering a sense of community and mutual encouragement that strengthens their faith. Hebrews 10:24-25 emphasizes the importance of this support: "And let us consider one another to provoke unto love and to good works: Not forsaking the assembling of ourselves together, as the manner of some is; but exhorting one another: and so much the more, as ye see the day approaching." By engaging in practices such as prayer, fellowship, and acts of service, Christians can build a supportive community where everyone feels valued and encouraged. Both wrestlers and Christians benefit from having mentors and role models, offering support to others, working together toward common goals, and being adaptable and open to receiving support. By investing time and effort into building strong relationships and giving back to their community, individuals in both contexts can create a positive, supportive environment that helps them achieve their goals and fulfill their purpose, ultimately bringing glory to God and experiencing the rewards of their perseverance and dedication.

Chapter 10 Strategy

Strategy is essential in both wrestling and the Christian life, involving careful planning, thoughtful execution, and the use of wisdom to achieve success. In wrestling, athletes use strategy to win matches by understanding their opponents' strengths and weaknesses, devising plans to counter their moves, and employing techniques that play to their own strengths. Wrestlers spend countless hours training, not only to build physical strength and agility but also to develop their tactical skills. They study their opponents by watching videos of their past matches, analyzing their techniques, and identifying patterns in their behavior. This preparation helps wrestlers anticipate their opponents' moves and develop counter-strategies. During matches, wrestlers must stay focused and adapt their strategies as the situation evolves, making quick decisions to take advantage of opportunities and avoid pitfalls. A successful wrestler knows that brute strength alone is not enough; it is the combination of physical ability and strategic thinking that leads to victory.

Similarly, Christians use spiritual wisdom to navigate their lives, make decisions that align with God's will, and overcome challenges. Proverbs 2:6 highlights the source of this wisdom: "For the LORD giveth wisdom: out of his mouth cometh knowledge and understanding." This verse reminds believers that true wisdom comes from God, and it is through seeking His guidance that they can gain the understanding needed to live righteous and fulfilling lives. Christians are encouraged to develop a deep relationship with God through prayer, Bible study, and meditation on His Word. These practices help them discern God's will, understand His teachings, and apply them to their daily lives. By relying on spiritual wisdom, Christians can make decisions that honor God, avoid the pitfalls of sin, and lead lives that reflect their faith.

Both wrestlers and Christians understand the importance of preparation in developing effective strategies. Wrestlers prepare for their matches through rigorous training, studying their opponents, and practicing various techniques. This preparation helps them build the physical and mental strength needed to execute their strategies successfully. Similarly, Christians prepare for the challenges of life by immersing themselves in God's Word, seeking His guidance through prayer, and engaging in fellowship with other believers. This spiritual preparation equips them with the knowledge and wisdom needed to face life's difficulties and make decisions that align with God's will. Psalm 119:105 emphasizes the importance of God's Word in providing guidance: "Thy word is a lamp unto my feet, and a light unto my path." By studying the Bible, Christians can gain insight into God's character, His promises, and His instructions for living a righteous life.

Both wrestlers and Christians must also be adaptable, adjusting their strategies as needed based on the circumstances they face. In wrestling, matches can be unpredictable, and athletes must be able to adapt their strategies on the fly. This adaptability allows them to respond effectively to their opponents' moves and take advantage of unexpected opportunities. Similarly, Christians must be flexible in their spiritual journey, ready to adjust their plans and approaches as they seek God's guidance and encounter various challenges. Proverbs 3:5-6 encourages believers to trust in God's direction: "Trust in the LORD with all thine heart; and lean not unto thine own understanding. In all thy ways acknowledge him, and he shall direct thy paths." By being open to God's leading and willing to adapt their strategies, Christians can navigate their spiritual journey more effectively and grow in their faith.

Both wrestlers and Christians benefit from the support and guidance of mentors and advisors who help them develop and refine their strategies. In wrestling, coaches and experienced teammates play a crucial role in helping athletes improve their skills and develop effective strategies. They provide valuable feedback, share their knowledge and experience, and offer encouragement and motivation. Similarly, in the Christian life, mentors, pastors, and more mature believers provide spiritual guidance, support, and encouragement. They help others grow in their understanding of God's Word, develop spiritual disciplines, and apply biblical principles to their lives. This mentorship provides accountability and support, ensuring that believers stay on the right path and continue to grow in their faith. Hebrews 10:24-25 emphasizes the importance of mutual support and encouragement: "And let us consider one another to provoke unto love and to good works: Not forsaking the assembling of ourselves together, as the manner of some is; but exhorting one another: and so much the more, as ye see the day approaching."

Both wrestlers and Christians must also practice patience and persistence in developing and executing their strategies. In wrestling, success often requires long hours of training, repeated practice of techniques, and gradual improvement over time. Wrestlers must be patient, recognizing that progress may be slow and setbacks are inevitable. They must persist in their efforts, continually refining their strategies and working towards their goals. Similarly, Christians must be patient and persistent in their spiritual journey, understanding that growth in faith takes time and effort. They must continually seek God's guidance, apply His teachings to their lives, and trust in His timing. Galatians 6:9 encourages believers to remain steadfast: "And let us not be weary in well doing: for in due season we shall reap, if we faint not." By practicing patience and persistence, Christians can develop the spiritual wisdom and strength needed to navigate life's challenges and fulfill God's purposes.

Both wrestlers and Christians must also be aware of their strengths and weaknesses, using this self-awareness to develop effective strategies. In wrestling, athletes must understand their physical abilities, technical skills, and areas for improvement. This self-awareness helps them develop strategies that play to their strengths and address their weaknesses. Similarly, Christians must be aware of their spiritual strengths and weaknesses, seeking God's help to grow in areas where they are lacking and using their gifts and talents to serve others. By being honest with themselves and relying on God's guidance, believers can develop strategies that help them live lives that honor God and reflect their faith.

Both contexts emphasize the importance of discipline and consistency in executing strategies. Wrestlers follow strict training regimens and dietary plans, making sacrifices to stay in peak physical condition. This discipline helps them stay focused and committed to their goals, ensuring that they are prepared to execute their strategies successfully. Similarly, Christians practice spiritual disciplines such as prayer, Bible study, worship, and fellowship to stay connected to God and draw on His strength. This consistency helps them stay focused on their spiritual journey, making it easier to apply God's wisdom and guidance in their lives. 1 Corinthians 9:25-27 illustrates the importance of discipline: "And every man that striveth for the mastery is temperate in all things. Now they do it to obtain a corruptible crown; but we an incorruptible. I therefore so run, not as uncertainly; so fight I, not as one that beateth the air: But I keep under my body, and bring it into subjection: lest that by any means, when I have preached to others, I myself should be a castaway."

Both wrestlers and Christians must also recognize the importance of setting clear goals and developing plans to achieve them. In wrestling, athletes set specific goals for their training and competition, such as improving their techniques, building strength, or winning matches. These goals provide motivation and direction, helping them stay focused and committed to their training regimen. Similarly, Christians set spiritual goals, such as growing in their faith, developing a deeper understanding of God's Word, or serving others more effectively. These goals help believers stay focused on their spiritual journey and make intentional efforts to grow and improve. Philippians 3:14 encourages believers to press toward their spiritual goals: "I press toward the mark for the prize of the high calling of God in Christ Jesus." By setting clear goals and developing strategies to achieve them, both wrestlers and Christians can work towards their objectives with purpose and determination.

Both wrestlers and Christians must also be willing to learn from their experiences, using both successes and failures to refine their strategies. In wrestling, athletes analyze their performances, identify areas for improvement, and make necessary adjustments to their training and techniques. This continuous learning process helps them grow as wrestlers and develop more effective strategies for future matches. Similarly, Christians must reflect on their spiritual journey, learning from their experiences and seeking God's guidance to grow in their faith. They must be open to God's correction and willing to make changes in their lives to align more closely with His will. Proverbs 3:11-12 reminds believers of the importance of accepting God's discipline: "My son, despise not the chastening of the LORD; neither be weary of his correction: For whom the LORD loveth he correcteth; even as a father the son in whom he delighteth." By being open to learning and growth, Christians can develop the spiritual wisdom and strength needed to navigate life's challenges and fulfill God's purposes.

Both wrestlers and Christians must also be aware of the importance of teamwork and collaboration in developing and executing strategies. In wrestling, athletes often train with teammates, sharing knowledge, techniques, and encouragement. This collaboration helps wrestlers improve their skills and develop more effective strategies. Similarly, Christians benefit from the support and collaboration of their faith community. By working together, sharing insights, and encouraging one another, believers can grow in their faith and develop strategies that help them live lives that honor God. Ecclesiastes 4:9-10 highlights the value of collaboration: "Two are better than one; because they have a good reward for their labour. For if they fall, the one will lift up his fellow: but woe to him that is alone when he falleth; for he hath not another to help him up." By working together and supporting one another, both wrestlers and Christians can achieve greater success and fulfill their goals.

In conclusion, strategy is essential in both wrestling and the Christian life, involving careful planning, thoughtful execution, and the use of wisdom to achieve success. Wrestlers use strategy to win matches by understanding their opponents, devising plans to counter their moves, and employing techniques that play to their strengths. Similarly, Christians use spiritual wisdom to navigate their lives, make decisions that align with God's will, and overcome challenges. Proverbs 2:6 highlights the source of this wisdom: "For the LORD giveth wisdom: out of his

mouth cometh knowledge and understanding." By seeking God's guidance, engaging in spiritual disciplines, and relying on the support and collaboration of their faith community, Christians can develop and execute strategies that help them live lives that honor God and reflect their faith. Both wrestlers and Christians must be adaptable, patient, persistent, and disciplined in their efforts, setting clear goals and learning from their experiences to refine their strategies. By staying committed to their goals and relying on their respective sources of strength, individuals in both contexts can achieve success, fulfill their purpose, and ultimately bring glory to God.

Chapter 11 Battling Temptation

Battling temptation is a critical aspect of both wrestling and the Christian life, requiring discipline, integrity, and reliance on a higher power to make the right choices. In wrestling, athletes face the temptation to cheat or use shortcuts to gain an advantage. This could involve using banned substances to enhance performance, engaging in unsportsmanlike behavior, or exploiting loopholes in the rules. Wrestlers are constantly under pressure to win, and the desire to succeed can sometimes lead them to consider unethical actions. However, true champions understand the importance of integrity and fair play. They know that real success comes from hard work, dedication, and adherence to the rules. Coaches and mentors play a crucial role in instilling these values in wrestlers, emphasizing that victories achieved through dishonesty are hollow and ultimately damaging to their character and reputation. By resisting the temptation to cheat, wrestlers uphold the integrity of the sport and earn respect from their peers and fans.

Similarly, Christians face various temptations in their daily lives and must rely on their faith and God's strength to resist them. Temptations can take many forms, such as the lure of materialism, the desire for power, or the pull of unhealthy habits and relationships. These temptations can lead individuals away from God's path and into actions that harm themselves and others. James 4:7 provides clear guidance for Christians: "Submit yourselves therefore to God. Resist the devil, and he will flee from you." This verse highlights the importance of submitting to God's authority and relying on His power to resist temptation. By drawing close to God through prayer, Bible study, and worship, Christians can strengthen their resolve and gain the wisdom needed to make righteous choices.

Both wrestlers and Christians benefit from having strong support systems to help them resist temptation. In wrestling, coaches, teammates, and family members can provide encouragement, accountability, and guidance. They help wrestlers stay focused on their goals and remind them of the importance of integrity and hard work. Similarly, in the Christian life, fellowship with other believers is essential. The Christian community provides support, encouragement, and accountability, helping individuals stay strong in their faith and resist temptation. Hebrews 10:24-25 emphasizes the importance of gathering together and encouraging one another: "And let us consider one another to provoke unto love and to good works: Not forsaking the assembling of ourselves together, as the manner of some is; but exhorting one another: and so much the more, as ye see the day approaching." By participating in a supportive faith community, Christians can build strong relationships that help them stay committed to God's path.

Both wrestlers and Christians must also develop self-discipline to resist temptation effectively. Wrestlers need to maintain strict training regimens, follow dietary guidelines, and adhere to ethical standards, even when it's challenging. This discipline helps them stay focused on their goals and avoid shortcuts that could compromise their integrity. Similarly, Christians must practice spiritual disciplines such as prayer, Bible study, and worship to strengthen their relationship with God and fortify their resolve against temptation. By consistently engaging in these practices, believers can develop the spiritual strength needed to resist the devil and stay true to their faith.

Preparation is another key element in resisting temptation for both wrestlers and Christians. Wrestlers prepare for matches by training rigorously, studying their opponents, and developing strategies to overcome challenges. This preparation helps them build the physical and mental strength needed to perform ethically and successfully. Similarly, Christians prepare for spiritual battles by immersing themselves in God's Word, seeking His guidance through prayer, and growing in their faith. Ephesians 6:11-13 encourages believers to put on the full armor of God to stand against the devil's schemes: "Put on the whole armour of God, that ye may be able to stand against the wiles of the devil. For we wrestle not against flesh and blood, but against principalities, against powers, against the rulers of the darkness of this world, against spiritual wickedness in high places. Wherefore take unto you the whole armour of God, that ye may be able to withstand in the evil day, and having done all, to stand." By preparing spiritually, Christians can equip themselves to resist temptation and remain steadfast in their faith.

Both wrestlers and Christians must also be vigilant and aware of the potential for temptation. In wrestling, athletes must be mindful of situations where they might be tempted to cheat or cut corners, such as when they are under intense pressure to win or when they see others engaging in unethical behavior. By staying alert and recognizing these situations, wrestlers can make conscious decisions to uphold their integrity. Similarly, Christians must be aware of the situations and influences that could lead them into temptation. This awareness allows them to take proactive steps to avoid or resist these temptations, such as seeking accountability, removing themselves from harmful environments, or reinforcing their spiritual practices. 1 Peter 5:8 warns believers to be vigilant: "Be sober, be vigilant; because your adversary the devil, as a roaring lion, walketh about, seeking whom he may devour."

Both wrestlers and Christians must also be willing to seek help when facing temptation. In wrestling, athletes can turn to their coaches, teammates, or mentors for guidance and support. These individuals can offer valuable advice, encouragement, and accountability, helping wrestlers stay on the right path. Similarly, Christians can seek support from their faith community, pastors, or spiritual mentors when they are struggling with temptation. By sharing their struggles and seeking guidance, believers can receive the help they need to overcome temptation and grow in their faith. James 5:16

emphasizes the importance of confessing sins and praying for one another: "Confess your faults one to another, and pray one for another, that ye may be healed. The effectual fervent prayer of a righteous man availeth much."

Both wrestlers and Christians must also recognize the long-term consequences of giving in to temptation. In wrestling, cheating or using shortcuts may bring temporary success, but it ultimately undermines the athlete's integrity, reputation, and long-term goals. Similarly, for Christians, succumbing to temptation can lead to spiritual harm, damage relationships, and create a barrier between them and God. By keeping the long-term consequences in mind, both wrestlers and Christians can strengthen their resolve to resist temptation and stay true to their values.

Both wrestlers and Christians must also cultivate a mindset of perseverance and resilience. Wrestlers face numerous challenges and setbacks in their careers, and they must develop the mental toughness to push through these difficulties and stay committed to their goals. Similarly, Christians face various trials and temptations in their spiritual journey, and they must rely on their faith and God's strength to persevere. James 1:2-4 encourages believers to view trials as opportunities for growth: "My brethren, count it all joy when ye fall into divers temptations; Knowing this, that the trying of your faith worketh patience. But let patience have her perfect work, that ye may be perfect and entire, wanting nothing." By embracing a mindset of perseverance, Christians can overcome temptation and grow stronger in their faith.

Both wrestlers and Christians must also develop strategies to cope with and overcome temptation. Wrestlers may use techniques such as visualization, positive self-talk, and setting specific goals to stay focused and motivated. These strategies help them maintain their integrity and resist the temptation to cheat or take shortcuts. Similarly, Christians can develop spiritual strategies to resist temptation, such as memorizing Scripture, praying regularly, and seeking accountability from trusted friends or mentors. By using these strategies, believers can strengthen their resolve and rely on God's power to overcome temptation. Psalm 119:11 highlights the importance of internalizing God's Word: "Thy word have I hid in mine heart, that I might not sin against thee."

Both wrestlers and Christians must also be committed to ongoing personal and spiritual growth. In wrestling, athletes continually work to improve their skills, strength, and mental toughness. This commitment to growth helps them stay competitive and maintain their integrity. Similarly, Christians must be committed to growing in their faith, continually seeking God's guidance, and striving to live according to His will. By pursuing personal and spiritual growth, believers can build the strength and wisdom needed to resist temptation and remain faithful to God.

In both wrestling and the Christian life, the battle against temptation is ongoing and requires constant vigilance and effort. Wrestlers must remain committed to their training, stay focused on their goals, and uphold their integrity in every match. Similarly, Christians must continually seek God's guidance, rely on His strength, and stay connected to their faith community to resist temptation and grow in their faith. By staying vigilant and committed, both wrestlers and Christians can overcome temptation and achieve success in their respective journeys.

Both wrestlers and Christians must also be willing to make sacrifices to maintain their integrity and resist temptation. In wrestling, athletes may need to sacrifice personal comfort, leisure time, or social activities to stay dedicated to their training and ethical standards. Similarly, Christians may need to make sacrifices to avoid temptation and stay true to their faith, such as giving up certain habits, relationships, or opportunities that could lead them away from God. Romans 12:1 urges believers to offer themselves as living sacrifices: "I beseech you therefore, brethren, by the mercies of God, that ye present your bodies a living sacrifice, holy, acceptable unto God, which is your reasonable service." By being willing to make sacrifices, Christians can honor God and strengthen their resolve to resist temptation.

Both wrestlers and Christians must also cultivate a strong sense of identity and purpose. Wrestlers who have a clear understanding of their goals and values are better equipped to resist the temptation to cheat or take shortcuts. They know that true success comes from hard work, dedication, and integrity. Similarly, Christians who have a strong sense of their identity in Christ and their purpose in God's plan are better equipped to resist temptation and stay committed to their faith. Ephesians 2:10 reminds believers of their identity and purpose: "For we are his workmanship, created in Christ Jesus unto good works, which God hath before ordained that we should walk in them."

By understanding their identity and purpose, Christians can find the motivation and strength to resist temptation and live according to God's will.

In conclusion, battling temptation is a critical aspect of both wrestling and the Christian life, requiring discipline, integrity, and reliance on a higher power to make the right choices. Wrestlers face the temptation to cheat or use shortcuts to gain an advantage, but true champions understand the importance of integrity and fair play. Similarly, Christians face various temptations in their daily lives and must rely on their faith and God's strength to resist them. James 4:7 provides clear guidance for Christians: "Submit yourselves therefore to God. Resist the devil, and he will flee from you." By developing self-discipline, preparing spiritually, staying vigilant, seeking support, recognizing long-term consequences, cultivating perseverance, and making sacrifices, both wrestlers and Christians can overcome temptation and achieve success in their respective journeys. By staying committed to their values and relying on their respective sources of strength, individuals in both contexts can honor their commitments, uphold their integrity, and ultimately bring glory to God.

Chapter 13 Humility

Humility is a significant aspect of both wrestling and the Christian life, requiring individuals to recognize their limitations, learn from their experiences, and maintain a respectful and modest attitude. In wrestling, athletes often learn humility through defeat. Wrestling is a challenging and competitive sport where even the most skilled athletes can face losses. When wrestlers experience defeat, they are confronted with their own limitations and weaknesses. These moments can be humbling, as they force wrestlers to acknowledge that they are not invincible and that there is always room for improvement. Defeat teaches wrestlers to be gracious and respectful towards their opponents, understanding that everyone has strengths and weaknesses. Humble wrestlers use their losses as opportunities for growth, analyzing their performances to identify areas for improvement and working hard to overcome their shortcomings. This attitude of humility helps them stay grounded, focused, and motivated to continue improving. Humility also fosters a positive team environment, as wrestlers who are humble are more likely to support their teammates, share their knowledge, and contribute to the overall success of the team.

Similarly, Christians are called to practice humility before God. Humility in the Christian life involves recognizing that God is the ultimate authority and source of all wisdom, strength, and guidance. It means acknowledging one's own limitations and weaknesses, and relying on God's grace and power. James 4:10 emphasizes the importance of humility: "Humble yourselves in the sight of the Lord, and he shall lift you up." This verse reminds believers that by humbling themselves before God, they open themselves to His blessings and support. Humility in the Christian context also involves treating others with respect and kindness, recognizing that everyone is created in the image of God and deserving of love and compassion. By practicing humility, Christians can build stronger relationships, foster a sense of community, and reflect the character of Christ in their interactions with others.

Both wrestlers and Christians must cultivate humility through self-reflection and a willingness to learn from their experiences. In wrestling, athletes must regularly evaluate their performances, acknowledging their mistakes and areas for improvement. This self-reflection helps them stay humble and focused on their goals. Similarly, Christians are encouraged to examine their lives, confess their sins, and seek God's guidance for growth. This process of self-reflection helps believers remain humble and dependent on God. Psalm 139:23-24 illustrates the importance of self-examination: "Search me, O God, and know my heart: try me, and know my thoughts: And see if there be any wicked way in me, and lead me in the way everlasting." By regularly reflecting on their actions and attitudes, Christians can cultivate humility and align their lives more closely with God's will.

Both wrestlers and Christians must also be open to receiving feedback and guidance from others. In wrestling, coaches, teammates, and mentors provide valuable feedback that helps athletes improve their skills and strategies. Humble wrestlers are open to this feedback, recognizing that it is essential for their growth and development. They understand that accepting constructive criticism is a sign of strength, not weakness. Similarly, Christians benefit from the guidance and support of their faith community. Pastors, spiritual mentors, and fellow believers can offer insights, encouragement, and accountability that help individuals grow in their faith. Proverbs 19:20 highlights the importance of accepting guidance: "Hear counsel, and receive instruction, that thou mayest be wise in thy latter end." By being open to feedback and guidance, Christians can cultivate humility and continue growing in their relationship with God.

Both wrestlers and Christians must also recognize the importance of gratitude in cultivating humility. In wrestling, athletes should be grateful for their opportunities to compete, the support of their coaches and teammates, and the lessons they learn through both victories and defeats. This attitude of gratitude helps wrestlers stay humble and appreciative of the journey, rather than becoming overly focused on the outcomes. Similarly, Christians are called to be grateful for God's blessings, His guidance, and His grace. By maintaining an attitude of gratitude, believers can stay humble and recognize their dependence on God. 1 Thessalonians 5:18 encourages gratitude: "In every thing give thanks: for this is the will of God in Christ Jesus concerning you." By regularly expressing gratitude, Christians can cultivate humility and a deeper appreciation for God's work in their lives.

Both wrestlers and Christians must also practice humility in their interactions with others. In wrestling, athletes should treat their opponents, coaches, and teammates with respect and kindness, regardless of the outcome of the match. Humble wrestlers recognize that everyone is on their own journey and that mutual respect is essential for a positive and supportive environment. Similarly, Christians are called to treat others with love and compassion, reflecting the character of Christ in their interactions. Philippians 2:3-4 emphasizes the importance of humility in relationships: "Let nothing be done through strife or vainglory; but in lowliness of mind let each esteem other better than themselves. Look not every man on his own things, but every man also on the things of others." By practicing humility in their interactions, Christians can build strong, supportive relationships and create a positive impact on those around them.

Both wrestlers and Christians must also understand that humility involves acknowledging and valuing the contributions of others. In wrestling, athletes should recognize the efforts and support of their coaches, teammates, and family members who contribute to their success. This acknowledgment fosters a sense of gratitude and humility, as wrestlers understand that their achievements are not solely their own. Similarly, Christians should recognize and value the contributions of others in their faith community, understanding that each person plays a vital role in the body of Christ. Romans 12:4-5 illustrates this interconnectedness: "For as we have many members in one body, and all members have not the same office: So we, being many, are one body in Christ, and every one members one of another." By valuing and acknowledging the contributions of others, Christians can cultivate humility and build a stronger, more unified community.

Both wrestlers and Christians must also be willing to serve others as an expression of humility. In wrestling, athletes can serve their teammates by offering support, sharing their knowledge, and helping others improve. This attitude of service fosters a sense of camaraderie and mutual respect within the team. Similarly, Christians are called to serve others, following the example of Christ who demonstrated ultimate humility through His service and sacrifice. Mark 10:45 highlights Christ's example: "For even the Son of man came not to be ministered unto, but to minister, and to give his life a ransom for many." By serving others, Christians can cultivate humility and reflect the love and character of Christ.

Both wrestlers and Christians must also practice humility by being willing to admit their mistakes and seek forgiveness. In wrestling, athletes may make errors in their techniques or strategies, and humble wrestlers are willing to acknowledge these mistakes and learn from them. This attitude of humility helps them grow and improve. Similarly, Christians are called to confess their sins and seek God's forgiveness, recognizing their need for His grace and mercy. 1 John 1:9 emphasizes the importance of confession: "If we confess our sins, he is faithful and just to forgive us our sins, and to cleanse us from all unrighteousness." By admitting their mistakes and seeking forgiveness, Christians can cultivate humility and experience God's transformative grace.

Both wrestlers and Christians must also practice humility by being teachable and open to learning from others. In wrestling, athletes who are teachable are more likely to improve and succeed, as they are willing to learn new techniques and strategies from their coaches and teammates. This teachability is a sign of humility, as it demonstrates a willingness to acknowledge one's limitations and seek growth. Similarly, Christians are called to be teachable and open to learning from God's Word, the Holy Spirit, and other believers. Proverbs 9:9 highlights the importance of being teachable: "Give instruction to a wise man, and he will be yet wiser: teach a just man, and he will increase in learning." By being teachable, Christians can cultivate humility and grow in their faith.

Both wrestlers and Christians must also understand that true humility involves putting others before oneself. In wrestling, athletes can demonstrate humility by prioritizing the success and well-being of their team over individual accolades. This attitude fosters a sense of unity and collective achievement. Similarly, Christians are called to put others before themselves, reflecting the selfless love of Christ. Philippians 2:3-4 emphasizes this selflessness: "Let nothing be done through strife or vainglory; but in lowliness of mind let each esteem other better than themselves. Look not every man on his own things, but every man also on the things of others." By putting others first, Christians can cultivate humility and create a positive impact on those around them.

In conclusion, humility is a significant aspect of both wrestling and the Christian life, requiring individuals to recognize their limitations, learn from their experiences, and maintain a respectful and modest attitude. Wrestlers often learn humility through defeat, acknowledging their weaknesses and using their losses as opportunities for growth. Similarly, Christians are called to practice humility before God, recognizing their dependence on Him and treating others with love and respect. James 4:10 emphasizes the importance of humility:

"Humble yourselves in the sight of the Lord, and he shall lift you up." By engaging in self-reflection, being open to feedback, expressing gratitude, practicing humility in interactions, valuing the contributions of others, serving others, admitting mistakes, being teachable, and putting others before themselves, both wrestlers and Christians can cultivate humility and achieve success in their respective journeys. By staying committed to these principles and relying on their respective sources of strength, individuals in both contexts can honor their commitments, uphold their integrity, and ultimately bring glory to God.

Chapter 14 Dedication

Dedication is a vital quality in both wrestling and the Christian life, demanding a deep commitment, consistent effort, and a heart fully invested in the pursuit of one's goals. Wrestlers exhibit dedication to their sport by adhering to rigorous training schedules, maintaining strict diets, and constantly working to improve their techniques and physical conditioning. They wake up early for practice, spend countless hours in the gym, and push through pain and fatigue to become the best they can be. This dedication requires sacrifice, as wrestlers often forgo social activities, leisure time, and even comfort to focus on their training and competitions. They set goals, such as winning matches, improving their skills, or achieving a certain level of fitness, and they remain steadfast in their pursuit of these goals despite the challenges they face. The journey of a wrestler is marked by discipline and resilience, as they learn to overcome setbacks, injuries, and losses, using each experience as a stepping stone toward greater success. Coaches play a significant role in fostering this dedication, providing guidance, motivation, and support to help wrestlers stay on track and reach their potential.

Similarly, Christians are called to show dedication to their faith, committing their hearts and lives to following Jesus and living according to God's Word. This dedication is not a mere casual interest but a wholehearted devotion that permeates every aspect of a believer's life. Colossians 3:23 emphasizes the importance of this commitment: "And whatsoever ye do, do it heartily, as to the Lord, and not unto men." This verse encourages Christians to approach all their endeavors with sincerity and zeal, recognizing that their ultimate service is to God. Dedication in the Christian life involves regular prayer, studying the Bible, attending worship services, and participating in fellowship with other believers. Through these practices, Christians deepen their relationship with God, grow in their understanding of His will, and gain the strength and guidance needed to live out their faith in daily life.

Both wrestlers and Christians must demonstrate perseverance and resilience as part of their dedication. Wrestlers face physical and mental challenges that test their commitment to the sport. They endure grueling training sessions, cope with the pressure of competition, and bounce back from defeats. Their dedication is evident in their ability to keep going, even when the going gets tough. They learn to embrace the process of growth, understanding that setbacks are part of the journey and that perseverance leads to improvement and success. Similarly, Christians encounter various trials and temptations that test their faith. Dedication to the Christian life means remaining faithful to God even in the face of adversity. James 1:12 encourages believers with the promise of reward for their perseverance: "Blessed is the man that endureth temptation: for when he is tried, he shall receive the crown of life, which the Lord hath promised to them that love him." By staying dedicated to their faith, Christians can overcome challenges, grow stronger in their relationship with God, and receive His blessings.

Both wrestlers and Christians must also be disciplined in their daily routines to maintain their dedication. Wrestlers follow strict training schedules, balanced diets, and recovery plans to ensure they are always at their best. This discipline helps them stay focused and committed to their goals. They understand that consistency is key to improvement and success, and they are willing to make the necessary sacrifices to stay dedicated to their sport. Similarly, Christians practice spiritual disciplines such as prayer, Bible study, worship, and fellowship to nurture their faith and stay connected to God. These disciplines require commitment and effort, but they are essential for spiritual growth and maintaining a strong relationship with God. By incorporating these practices into their daily lives, Christians can stay dedicated to their faith and draw closer to God.

Both wrestlers and Christians benefit from having a support system to help them stay dedicated. Wrestlers rely on coaches, teammates, and family members for encouragement, guidance, and accountability. These support networks play a crucial role in helping wrestlers stay motivated, overcome challenges, and achieve their goals. Similarly, Christians rely on their faith community, including pastors, mentors, and fellow believers, for support and encouragement. The Christian community provides a network of relationships that offer prayer, guidance, and accountability, helping believers stay dedicated to their faith. Hebrews 10:24-25 emphasizes the importance of this mutual support: "And let us consider one another to provoke unto love and to good works: Not forsaking the assembling of ourselves together, as the manner of some is; but exhorting one another: and so much the more, as ye see the day approaching." By being part of a supportive community, Christians can strengthen their dedication to God and grow in their faith.

Both wrestlers and Christians must also set clear goals and work diligently to achieve them. Wrestlers set specific objectives for their training and competition, such as mastering a particular technique, reaching a certain weight class, or winning a championship. These goals provide motivation and direction, helping wrestlers stay focused and committed to their training regimen. They regularly evaluate their progress, adjust their strategies, and continue working toward their goals with unwavering dedication. Similarly, Christians set spiritual goals, such as growing in their knowledge of the Bible, developing a deeper prayer life, or serving others more effectively. These goals help believers stay focused on their spiritual journey and make intentional efforts to grow in their faith. Philippians 3:14 captures the essence of this pursuit: "I press toward the mark for the prize of the high calling of God in Christ Jesus." By setting clear goals and working diligently to achieve them, both wrestlers and Christians can stay dedicated to their respective journeys.

Both wrestlers and Christians must also be willing to make sacrifices to maintain their dedication. Wrestlers often sacrifice personal comfort, leisure time, and social activities to stay committed to their training and competition schedules. These sacrifices are necessary to achieve their goals and succeed in their sport. Similarly, Christians may need to make sacrifices to stay dedicated to their faith, such as giving up certain habits, relationships, or opportunities that could lead them away from God. Romans 12:1 urges believers to offer themselves as living sacrifices: "I beseech you therefore, brethren, by the mercies of God, that ye present your bodies a living sacrifice, holy, acceptable unto God, which is your reasonable service." By being willing to make sacrifices, Christians can honor God and strengthen their dedication to Him.

Both wrestlers and Christians must also recognize the importance of staying motivated and inspired. Wrestlers often draw motivation from their passion for the sport, their desire to achieve their goals, and the support of their coaches and teammates. They find inspiration in the successes of others, the progress they see in themselves, and the thrill of competition. Similarly, Christians can find motivation and inspiration in their relationship with God, the teachings of the Bible, and the support of their faith community. They draw strength from God's promises, the examples of faithful believers, and the hope of eternal life. Colossians 3:23 encourages Christians to stay motivated in all their endeavors: "And whatsoever ye do, do it heartily, as to the Lord, and not unto men." By staying motivated and inspired, Christians can maintain their dedication to God and continue growing in their faith.

Both wrestlers and Christians must also be open to continuous learning and improvement. Wrestlers are always looking for ways to improve their techniques, increase their strength, and enhance their performance. They seek feedback from their coaches, study their opponents, and learn from their experiences. This commitment to continuous learning helps them stay dedicated to their sport and achieve greater success. Similarly, Christians are called to continually grow in their knowledge of God's Word, deepen their understanding of His will, and develop their spiritual gifts. They seek wisdom through prayer, Bible study, and the guidance of the Holy Spirit. Proverbs 9:9 highlights the importance of continuous learning: "Give instruction to a wise man, and he will be yet wiser: teach a just man, and he will increase in learning." By being open to continuous learning and improvement, Christians can maintain their dedication to God and grow in their faith.

Both wrestlers and Christians must also practice patience and perseverance as part of their dedication. Wrestlers understand that success does not come overnight and that it takes time, effort, and persistence to achieve their goals. They learn to be patient with themselves, embracing the process of growth and improvement. Similarly, Christians must be patient and persevere in their faith journey, understanding that spiritual growth takes time and effort. They trust in God's timing and remain steadfast in their commitment to Him, even when faced with challenges and setbacks. Galatians 6:9 encourages believers to remain steadfast: "And let us not be weary in well doing: for in due season we shall reap, if we faint not." By practicing patience and perseverance, Christians can maintain their dedication to God and continue growing in their faith.

Both wrestlers and Christians must also cultivate a strong sense of purpose and identity. Wrestlers who have a clear understanding of their goals and values are better equipped to stay dedicated to their sport. They know why they are training, what they want to achieve, and what they stand for. This sense of purpose drives their dedication and keeps them focused on their goals. Similarly, Christians who have a strong sense of their identity in Christ and their purpose in God's plan are better equipped to stay dedicated to their faith. They understand that their ultimate goal is to glorify God and fulfill His purposes for their lives. Ephesians 2:10 reminds believers of their identity and purpose:

"For we are his workmanship, created in Christ Jesus unto good works, which God hath before ordained that we should walk in them." By understanding their purpose and identity, Christians can find the motivation and strength to stay dedicated to God and live according to His will.

In conclusion, dedication is a vital quality in both wrestling and the Christian life, demanding a deep commitment, consistent effort, and a heart fully invested in the pursuit of one's goals. Wrestlers exhibit dedication to their sport by adhering to rigorous training schedules, maintaining strict diets, and constantly working to improve their techniques and physical conditioning. Similarly, Christians show dedication

to their faith by committing their hearts and lives to following Jesus and living according to God's Word. Colossians 3:23 emphasizes the importance of this commitment: "And whatsoever ye do, do it heartily, as to the Lord, and not unto men." By demonstrating perseverance, discipline, setting clear goals, making sacrifices, staying motivated, embracing continuous learning, practicing patience, and cultivating a strong sense of purpose, both wrestlers and Christians can maintain their dedication and achieve success in their respective journeys. By staying committed to their values and relying on their respective sources of strength, individuals in both contexts can honor their commitments, uphold their integrity, and ultimately bring glory to God.

Chapter 15 Mental Toughness

Mental toughness is a crucial aspect of both wrestling and the Christian life, requiring individuals to develop resilience, perseverance, and a strong mindset to overcome challenges and achieve their goals. In wrestling, mental toughness is just as important as physical strength and skill. Wrestlers face intense physical and mental demands during training and competition. They must push through fatigue, pain, and the pressure to perform at their best. Developing mental toughness helps wrestlers stay focused, maintain a positive attitude, and keep fighting even when the odds are against them. This mental resilience is built through rigorous training, learning to cope with setbacks, and cultivating a mindset that embraces challenges as opportunities for growth. Coaches play a significant role in fostering mental toughness, teaching wrestlers techniques to manage stress, visualize success, and stay motivated. Wrestlers learn to set goals, stay disciplined, and develop the ability to stay calm under pressure. This mental fortitude not only helps them in the sport but also equips them with valuable skills for life outside the wrestling mat.

Similarly, Christians develop spiritual resilience by relying on their faith and God's strength to navigate the difficulties of life. Spiritual resilience involves trusting in God's promises, maintaining hope and peace in the face of adversity, and drawing strength from a deep relationship with God. Philippians 4:6-7 offers a powerful reminder of the source of this resilience: "Be careful for nothing; but in every thing by prayer and supplication with thanksgiving let your requests be made known unto God. And the peace of God, which passeth all understanding, shall keep your hearts and minds through Christ Jesus." This verse encourages Christians to bring their worries and challenges to God in prayer, trusting that He will provide peace and guidance. By focusing on God's faithfulness and His ability to work in their lives, believers can develop a resilient spirit that withstands the trials and tribulations they encounter.

Both wrestlers and Christians build resilience by facing and overcoming challenges. Wrestlers encounter numerous obstacles, such as tough opponents, injuries, and the physical demands of training. Each challenge provides an opportunity to develop greater mental toughness. Wrestlers learn to push through pain, stay committed to their goals, and use setbacks as motivation to improve. This process of overcoming challenges helps them build confidence and a resilient mindset. Similarly, Christians face various trials and temptations that test their faith. Spiritual resilience is developed through experiences that challenge their beliefs and reliance on God. By trusting in God's strength and remaining faithful through difficult times, Christians grow stronger in their faith and develop the ability to persevere. James 1:2-4 speaks to this process: "My brethren, count it all joy when ye fall into divers temptations; Knowing this, that the trying of your faith worketh patience. But let patience have her perfect work, that ye may be perfect and entire, wanting nothing."

Both wrestlers and Christians must also practice self-discipline and consistency to build mental toughness and spiritual resilience. Wrestlers follow strict training regimens, maintain healthy diets, and continually work on their techniques. This discipline helps them stay focused and committed to their goals, even when the going gets tough. Similarly, Christians practice spiritual disciplines such as prayer, Bible study, worship, and fellowship to stay connected to God and draw on His strength. These practices help them develop a resilient spirit that can withstand the pressures and challenges of life. By consistently engaging in these disciplines, believers build a strong foundation of faith that supports them in difficult times.

Both wrestlers and Christians benefit from the support and encouragement of others as they develop resilience. Wrestlers rely on coaches, teammates, and family members for motivation, guidance, and support. This support network helps them stay focused, overcome obstacles, and keep pushing forward. Similarly, Christians rely on their faith community for encouragement, prayer, and accountability. The support of fellow believers provides strength and comfort, helping individuals stay resilient in their faith. Hebrews 10:24-25 emphasizes the importance of this mutual support: "And let us consider one another to provoke unto love and to good works: Not forsaking the assembling of ourselves together, as the manner of some is; but exhorting one another: and so much the more, as ye see the day approaching." By being part of a supportive community, Christians can draw on the collective strength and encouragement of others to build their spiritual resilience.

Both wrestlers and Christians must also develop the ability to stay focused and maintain a positive mindset in the face of adversity. Wrestlers learn to focus on their goals, visualize success, and stay positive even when they are physically and mentally exhausted. This mental focus helps them stay determined and motivated, enabling them to perform at their best. Similarly, Christians are encouraged to focus on God's promises, maintain a positive outlook, and trust in His plans for their lives. Philippians 4:8 encourages believers to focus on positive and uplifting things: "Finally, brethren, whatsoever things are true, whatsoever things are honest, whatsoever things are just, whatsoever things are pure, whatsoever things are lovely, whatsoever things are of good report; if there be any virtue, and if there be any praise, think on these things." By keeping their minds focused on God's goodness and His promises, Christians can maintain a resilient spirit that withstands life's challenges.

Both wrestlers and Christians must also develop coping strategies to manage stress and anxiety. Wrestlers use techniques such as deep breathing, visualization, and positive self-talk to stay calm and focused during competitions. These coping strategies help them manage the pressure and perform at their best. Similarly, Christians use prayer, meditation on Scripture, and fellowship with other believers to manage stress and find peace in God's presence. By bringing their concerns to God in prayer and trusting in His care, believers can experience the peace that surpasses understanding, as described in Philippians 4:7. This peace helps them stay resilient and focused, even in the face of difficulties.

Both wrestlers and Christians must also embrace the process of growth and improvement. Wrestlers understand that developing mental toughness is a journey that requires time, effort, and perseverance. They embrace the process of training, learning from their experiences, and continually striving to improve. Similarly, Christians recognize that spiritual resilience is developed over time through a deepening relationship with God and ongoing spiritual growth. They embrace the journey of faith, seeking to grow closer to God and become more like Christ. 2 Peter 3:18 encourages believers to grow in their faith: "But grow in grace, and in the knowledge of our Lord and Saviour Jesus Christ. To him be glory both now and for ever. Amen." By embracing the process of growth, both wrestlers and Christians can develop the resilience needed to overcome challenges and achieve their goals.

Both wrestlers and Christians must also practice gratitude and maintain a thankful heart. Wrestlers who cultivate gratitude for their opportunities, experiences, and the support they receive are better equipped to stay positive and resilient. Gratitude helps them maintain a balanced perspective and appreciate the journey, rather than focusing solely on outcomes. Similarly, Christians are called to be thankful in all circumstances, recognizing God's blessings and His presence in their lives. 1 Thessalonians 5:18 encourages believers to give thanks: "In every thing give thanks: for this is the will of God in Christ Jesus concerning you." By practicing gratitude, Christians can cultivate a resilient spirit that trusts in God's goodness and remains hopeful even in difficult times.

Both wrestlers and Christians must also be willing to seek help and support when needed. Wrestlers often turn to their coaches, sports psychologists, and mentors for guidance and support in developing mental toughness. These individuals provide valuable insights, encouragement, and strategies to help wrestlers stay focused and resilient. Similarly, Christians are encouraged to seek support from their faith community, pastors, and spiritual mentors when they face challenges. By sharing their struggles and seeking prayer and guidance, believers can find the strength and encouragement they need to stay resilient in their faith. Galatians 6:2 emphasizes the importance of bearing one another's burdens: "Bear ye one another's burdens, and so fulfil the law of Christ." By seeking help and support, both wrestlers and Christians can build a strong foundation of resilience.

Both wrestlers and Christians must also recognize the importance of rest and recovery in building resilience. Wrestlers understand that rest is essential for physical and mental recovery, helping them stay strong and perform at their best. They prioritize rest and recovery as part of their training regimen, knowing that it is crucial for long-term success. Similarly, Christians need periods of rest and spiritual renewal to maintain their resilience and grow in their faith. Jesus Himself took time to rest and pray, setting an example for His followers. Matthew 11:28-30 offers an invitation to rest: "Come unto me, all ye that labour and are heavy laden, and I will give you rest. Take my yoke upon you, and learn of me; for I am meek and lowly in heart: and ye shall find rest unto your souls. For my yoke is easy, and my burden is light." By taking time to rest in God's presence, Christians can renew their spiritual strength and find peace.

Both wrestlers and Christians must also develop a strong sense of purpose and identity. Wrestlers who have a clear understanding of their goals and values are better equipped to stay resilient in the face of challenges. They know why they are training and what they want to achieve, which helps them stay motivated and focused. Similarly,

Christians who have a strong sense of their identity in Christ and their purpose in God's plan are better equipped to stay resilient in their faith. They understand that their ultimate goal is to glorify God and fulfill His purposes for their lives. Ephesians 2:10 reminds believers of their identity and purpose: "For we are his workmanship, created in Christ Jesus unto good works, which God hath before ordained that we should walk in them." By understanding their purpose and identity, Christians can find the motivation and strength to stay resilient and live according to God's will.

In conclusion, mental toughness is a crucial aspect of both wrestling and the Christian life, requiring individuals to develop resilience, perseverance, and a

strong mindset to overcome challenges and achieve their goals. Wrestlers develop mental toughness through rigorous training, learning to cope with setbacks, and cultivating a mindset that embraces challenges as opportunities for growth. Similarly, Christians develop spiritual resilience by relying on their faith and God's strength to navigate the difficulties of life. Philippians 4:6-7 offers a powerful reminder of the source of this resilience: "Be careful for nothing; but in every thing by prayer and supplication with thanksgiving let your requests be made known unto God. And the peace of God, which passeth all understanding, shall keep your hearts and minds through Christ Jesus." By practicing self-discipline, seeking support, staying focused, embracing growth, practicing gratitude, seeking help, prioritizing rest, and understanding their purpose and identity, both wrestlers and Christians can build the resilience needed to overcome challenges and achieve their goals. By staying committed to these principles and relying on their respective sources of strength, individuals in both contexts can honor their commitments, uphold their integrity, and ultimately bring glory to God.

Chapter 16 Consistency

Consistency is crucial in both wrestling and the Christian life, demanding regular practice, unwavering dedication, and steadfast commitment to continual improvement and faithful living. In wrestling, athletes understand that consistent practice is the key to mastering techniques, building strength, and developing the mental toughness needed to succeed. Wrestlers engage in daily training sessions that include drills, conditioning exercises, and sparring matches. These practices are designed to hone their skills, increase their endurance, and prepare them for the physical and mental demands of competition. The routine of consistent practice helps wrestlers develop muscle memory, improve their reflexes, and become more proficient in executing moves. It also instills discipline, as wrestlers learn to push through fatigue, pain, and setbacks, knowing that perseverance will lead to progress. Coaches play a vital role in this process, providing guidance, feedback, and motivation to ensure that wrestlers stay on track and continue to advance. The commitment to consistent practice not only enhances physical capabilities but also builds character, resilience, and a strong work ethic, qualities that benefit wrestlers both on and off the mat.

Similarly, Christians are called to practice their faith consistently, engaging in regular spiritual disciplines that nurture their relationship with God and strengthen their faith. Consistent practice of faith involves daily prayer, reading and studying the Bible, attending worship services, and participating in fellowship with other believers. These practices help Christians grow in their understanding of God's Word, deepen their spiritual lives, and remain steadfast in their commitment to living according to God's will. 1 Corinthians 15:58 emphasizes the importance of being steadfast and unmovable in faith: "Therefore, my beloved brethren, be ye stedfast, unmoveable, always abounding in the work of the Lord, forasmuch as ye know that your labour is not in vain in the Lord." This verse encourages believers to remain faithful and diligent, assuring them that their efforts are meaningful and valued by God. By practicing their faith consistently, Christians can develop a strong spiritual foundation that helps them navigate life's challenges and remain faithful to God's calling.

Both wrestlers and Christians benefit from the structure and discipline that consistent practice provides. For wrestlers, adhering to a regular training schedule ensures that they are continually improving and staying in peak physical condition. This discipline helps them maintain focus, set and achieve goals, and prepare effectively for competitions. Consistent practice also helps wrestlers build confidence, as they see the results of their hard work and dedication over time. Similarly, Christians benefit from the routine of regular spiritual disciplines, which help them stay connected to God and grounded in their faith. Daily prayer and Bible study provide spiritual nourishment, guidance, and strength, while regular worship and fellowship offer encouragement, accountability, and support from the faith community. This consistent practice helps Christians build a resilient faith that can withstand the pressures and trials of life.

Both wrestlers and Christians must also embrace the idea of incremental progress, understanding that consistent practice leads to gradual but meaningful improvement. Wrestlers recognize that mastery of techniques and physical conditioning does not happen overnight; it requires patience, persistence, and a willingness to learn from each practice session. They celebrate small victories and improvements, knowing that these incremental gains contribute to their overall success. Similarly, Christians understand that spiritual growth is a lifelong journey that involves continuous learning, reflection, and application of God's teachings. They embrace the process of growing in faith, celebrating milestones in their spiritual journey and remaining committed to ongoing development. Philippians 1:6 offers encouragement for this journey: "Being confident of this very thing, that he which hath begun a good work in you will perform it until the day of Jesus Christ." By valuing incremental progress, both wrestlers and Christians can stay motivated and dedicated to their respective paths.

Both wrestlers and Christians also learn the importance of perseverance through consistent practice. Wrestlers face numerous challenges, including physical exhaustion, injuries, and tough competition. Consistent practice teaches them to persevere through these difficulties, developing mental toughness and resilience. They learn to push through pain, stay focused on their goals, and keep moving forward even when progress seems slow. Similarly, Christians encounter trials and temptations that test their faith and commitment. Consistent practice of spiritual disciplines helps them persevere, finding strength in God and relying on His promises. Romans 5:3-4 speaks to this process: "And not only so, but we glory in tribulations also: knowing that tribulation worketh patience; And patience, experience; and experience, hope." By persevering through challenges, Christians build a stronger, more resilient faith.

Both wrestlers and Christians also understand the importance of accountability in maintaining consistent practice. Wrestlers rely on their coaches, teammates, and training partners to keep them accountable, provide feedback, and offer support. This accountability helps them stay committed to their training regimen and continue improving. Similarly, Christians benefit from the accountability provided by their faith community. Fellow believers, pastors, and mentors can offer encouragement, guidance, and support, helping individuals stay committed to their spiritual practices and grow in their faith. Hebrews 10:24-25 highlights the value of mutual encouragement: "And let us consider one another to provoke unto love and to good works: Not forsaking the assembling of ourselves together, as the manner of some is; but exhorting one another: and so much the more, as ye see the day approaching." By fostering accountability, both wrestlers and Christians can maintain their dedication and continue progressing in their respective journeys.

Both wrestlers and Christians also recognize the importance of setting goals and working diligently to achieve them. Wrestlers set specific, measurable goals for their training and competition, such as improving their techniques, increasing their strength, or winning matches. These goals provide motivation and direction, helping them stay focused and committed to their practice. They regularly evaluate their progress, adjust their strategies, and continue working towards their goals with determination. Similarly, Christians set spiritual goals, such as deepening their understanding of the Bible, enhancing their prayer life, or serving others more effectively. These goals help believers stay focused on their spiritual journey and make intentional efforts to grow in their faith. Philippians 3:14 captures this pursuit: "I press toward the mark for the prize of the high calling of God in Christ Jesus." By setting and pursuing clear goals, both wrestlers and Christians can stay motivated and dedicated to their paths.

Both wrestlers and Christians must also be willing to make sacrifices to maintain consistent practice. Wrestlers often sacrifice personal comfort, leisure time, and social activities to stay dedicated to their training. These sacrifices are necessary to achieve their goals and succeed in their sport. Similarly, Christians may need to make sacrifices to stay committed to their faith, such as giving up certain habits, relationships, or opportunities that could lead them away from God. Romans 12:1 urges believers to offer themselves as living sacrifices: "I beseech you therefore, brethren, by the mercies of God, that ye present your bodies a living sacrifice, holy, acceptable unto God, which is your reasonable service." By being willing to make sacrifices, Christians can honor God and strengthen their dedication to Him.

Both wrestlers and Christians also understand the importance of staying motivated and inspired. Wrestlers often draw motivation from their passion for the sport, their desire to achieve their goals, and the support of their coaches and teammates. They find inspiration in the successes of others, the progress they see in themselves, and the thrill of competition. Similarly, Christians find motivation and inspiration in their relationship with God, the teachings of the Bible, and the support of their faith community. They draw strength from God's promises, the examples of faithful believers, and the hope of eternal life. Colossians 3:23 encourages Christians to stay motivated in all their endeavors: "And whatsoever ye do, do it heartily, as to the Lord, and not unto men." By staying motivated and inspired, Christians can maintain their dedication to God and continue growing in their faith.

Both wrestlers and Christians must also be open to continuous learning and improvement. Wrestlers are always looking for ways to improve their techniques, increase their strength, and enhance their performance. They seek feedback from their coaches, study their opponents, and learn from their experiences. This commitment to continuous learning helps them stay dedicated to their sport and achieve greater success. Similarly, Christians are called to continually grow in their knowledge of God's Word, deepen their understanding of His will, and develop their spiritual gifts. They seek wisdom through prayer, Bible study, and the guidance of the Holy Spirit. Proverbs 9:9 highlights the importance of continuous learning: "Give instruction to a wise man, and he will be yet wiser: teach a just man, and he will increase in learning." By being open to continuous learning and improvement, Christians can maintain their dedication to God and grow in their faith.

Both wrestlers and Christians must also practice patience and perseverance as part of their dedication. Wrestlers understand that success does not come overnight and that it takes time, effort, and persistence to achieve their goals. They learn to be patient with themselves, embracing the process of growth and improvement. Similarly, Christians must be patient and persevere in their faith journey, understanding that spiritual growth takes time and effort.

They trust in God's timing and remain steadfast in their commitment to Him, even when faced with challenges and setbacks. Galatians 6:9 encourages believers to remain steadfast: "And let us not be weary in well doing: for in due season we shall reap, if we faint not." By practicing patience and perseverance, Christians can maintain their dedication to God and continue growing in their faith.

Both wrestlers and Christians must also cultivate a strong sense of purpose and identity. Wrestlers who have a clear understanding of their goals and values are better equipped to stay dedicated to their sport. They know why they are training, what they want to achieve, and what they stand for. This sense of purpose drives their dedication and keeps them focused on their goals. Similarly, Christians who have a strong sense of their identity in Christ and their purpose in God's plan are better equipped to stay dedicated to their faith.

They understand that their ultimate goal is to glorify God and fulfill His purposes for their lives. Ephesians 2:10 reminds believers of their identity and purpose: "For we are his workmanship, created in Christ Jesus unto good works, which God hath before ordained that we should walk in them." By understanding their purpose and identity, Christians can find the motivation and strength to stay dedicated to God and live according to His will.

In conclusion, consistency is crucial in both wrestling and the Christian life, demanding regular practice, unwavering dedication, and steadfast commitment to continual improvement and faithful living. Wrestlers exhibit dedication to their sport by adhering to rigorous training schedules, maintaining strict diets, and constantly working to improve their techniques and physical conditioning. Similarly, Christians show dedication to their faith by committing their hearts and lives to following Jesus and living according to God's Word. 1 Corinthians 15:58 emphasizes the importance of being steadfast and unmovable in faith: "Therefore, my beloved brethren, be ye stedfast, unmoveable, always abounding in the work of the Lord, forasmuch as ye know that your labour is not in vain in the Lord." By demonstrating perseverance, discipline, setting clear goals, making sacrifices, staying motivated, embracing continuous learning, practicing patience, and cultivating a strong sense of purpose, both wrestlers and Christians can maintain their dedication and achieve success in their respective journeys. By staying committed to their values and relying on their respective sources of strength, individuals in both contexts can honor their commitments, uphold their integrity, and ultimately bring glory to God.

Chapter 17 Focus on the Goal

Focus on the goal is essential in both wrestling and the Christian life, requiring unwavering determination, clear vision, and a steadfast commitment to achieving one's objectives. In wrestling, athletes must focus on winning matches and achieving success in their sport. This focus drives them to train rigorously, maintain strict diets, and continually work to improve their techniques and physical conditioning. Wrestlers set specific goals, such as winning a championship, improving their skills, or reaching a certain level of fitness, and they remain dedicated to these goals despite the challenges they face. The journey of a wrestler is marked by discipline and resilience, as they learn to overcome setbacks, injuries, and losses, using each experience as a stepping stone toward greater success. Coaches play a vital role in helping wrestlers maintain their focus, providing guidance, motivation, and support to ensure that they stay on track and continue to advance. By keeping their eyes on the prize, wrestlers can stay motivated, push through difficult times, and ultimately achieve their goals.

Similarly, Christians are called to focus on the goal of eternal life, committing their hearts and lives to following Jesus and living according to God's Word. This focus is not a mere casual interest but a wholehearted devotion that shapes every aspect of a believer's life. Philippians 3:14 emphasizes the importance of this commitment: "I press toward the mark for the prize of the high calling of God in Christ Jesus." This verse encourages Christians to remain steadfast in their pursuit of the ultimate goal, recognizing that their efforts are meaningful and valued by God. Focusing on eternal life involves regular prayer, reading and studying the Bible, attending worship services, and participating in fellowship with other believers. These practices help Christians grow in their understanding of God's Word, deepen their spiritual lives, and remain steadfast in their commitment to living according to God's will.

Both wrestlers and Christians benefit from the structure and discipline that comes with focusing on their goals. For wrestlers, adhering to a regular training schedule ensures that they are continually improving and staying in peak physical condition. This discipline helps them maintain focus, set and achieve goals, and prepare effectively for competitions. Consistent practice also helps wrestlers build confidence, as they see the results of their hard work and dedication over time. Similarly, Christians benefit from the routine of regular spiritual disciplines, which help them stay connected to God and grounded in their faith. Daily prayer and Bible study provide spiritual nourishment, guidance, and strength, while regular worship and fellowship offer encouragement, accountability, and support from the faith community. This consistent practice helps Christians build a resilient faith that can withstand the pressures and trials of life.

Both wrestlers and Christians must also embrace the idea of incremental progress, understanding that focusing on the goal leads to gradual but meaningful improvement. Wrestlers recognize that mastery of techniques and physical conditioning does not happen overnight; it requires patience, persistence, and a willingness to learn from each practice session. They celebrate small victories and improvements, knowing that these incremental gains contribute to their overall success. Similarly, Christians understand that spiritual growth is a lifelong journey that involves continuous learning, reflection, and application of God's teachings. They embrace the process of growing in faith, celebrating milestones in their spiritual journey and remaining committed to ongoing development. Philippians 1:6 offers encouragement for this journey: "Being confident of this very thing, that he which hath begun a good work in you will perform it until the day of Jesus Christ." By valuing incremental progress, both wrestlers and Christians can stay motivated and dedicated to their respective paths.

Both wrestlers and Christians also learn the importance of perseverance through focusing on their goals. Wrestlers face numerous challenges, including physical exhaustion, injuries, and tough competition. Focusing on their goals teaches them to persevere through these difficulties, developing mental toughness and resilience. They learn to push through pain, stay committed to their goals, and keep moving forward even when progress seems slow. Similarly, Christians encounter trials and temptations that test their faith and commitment. Focusing on the goal of eternal life helps them persevere, finding strength in God and relying on His promises. Romans 5:3-4 speaks to this process: "And not only so, but we glory in tribulations also: knowing that tribulation worketh patience; And patience, experience; and experience, hope." By persevering through challenges, Christians build a stronger, more resilient faith.

Both wrestlers and Christians also understand the importance of accountability in maintaining focus on their goals. Wrestlers rely on their coaches, teammates, and training partners to keep them accountable, provide feedback, and offer support. This accountability helps them stay committed to their training regimen and continue improving. Similarly, Christians benefit from the accountability provided by their faith community. Fellow believers, pastors, and mentors can offer encouragement, guidance, and support, helping individuals stay committed to their spiritual practices and grow in their faith. Hebrews 10:24-25 highlights the value of mutual encouragement: "And let us consider one another to provoke unto love and to good works: Not forsaking the assembling of ourselves together, as the manner of some is; but exhorting one another: and so much the more, as ye see the day approaching." By fostering accountability, both wrestlers and Christians can maintain their dedication and continue progressing in their respective journeys.

Both wrestlers and Christians also recognize the importance of setting goals and working diligently to achieve them. Wrestlers set specific, measurable goals for their training and competition, such as improving their techniques, increasing their strength, or winning matches. These goals provide motivation and direction, helping them stay focused and committed to their practice. They regularly evaluate their progress, adjust their strategies, and continue working towards their goals with determination. Similarly, Christians set spiritual goals, such as deepening their understanding of the Bible, enhancing their prayer life, or serving others more effectively. These goals help believers stay focused on their spiritual journey and make intentional efforts to grow in their faith. Philippians 3:14 captures this pursuit: "I press toward the mark for the prize of the high calling of God in Christ Jesus." By setting and pursuing clear goals, both wrestlers and Christians can stay motivated and dedicated to their paths.

Both wrestlers and Christians must also be willing to make sacrifices to maintain their focus on their goals. Wrestlers often sacrifice personal comfort, leisure time, and social activities to stay dedicated to their training. These sacrifices are necessary to achieve their goals and succeed in their sport. Similarly, Christians may need to make sacrifices to stay committed to their faith, such as giving up certain habits, relationships, or opportunities that could lead them away from God. Romans 12:1 urges believers to offer themselves as living sacrifices: "I beseech you therefore, brethren, by the mercies of God, that ye present your bodies a living sacrifice, holy, acceptable unto God, which is your reasonable service." By being willing to make sacrifices, Christians can honor God and strengthen their dedication to Him.

Both wrestlers and Christians also understand the importance of staying motivated and inspired. Wrestlers often draw motivation from their passion for the sport, their desire to achieve their goals, and the support of their coaches and teammates. They find inspiration in the successes of others, the progress they see in themselves, and the thrill of competition. Similarly, Christians find motivation and inspiration in their relationship with God, the teachings of the Bible, and the support of their faith community. They draw strength from God's promises, the examples of faithful believers, and the hope of eternal life. Colossians 3:23 encourages Christians to stay motivated in all their endeavors: "And whatsoever ye do, do it heartily, as to the Lord, and not unto men." By staying motivated and inspired, Christians can maintain their dedication to God and continue growing in their faith.

Both wrestlers and Christians must also be open to continuous learning and improvement. Wrestlers are always looking for ways to improve their techniques, increase their strength, and enhance their performance. They seek feedback from their coaches, study their opponents, and learn from their experiences. This commitment to continuous learning helps them stay dedicated to their sport and achieve greater success. Similarly, Christians are called to continually grow in their knowledge of God's Word, deepen their understanding of His will, and develop their spiritual gifts. They seek wisdom through prayer, Bible study, and the guidance of the Holy Spirit. Proverbs 9:9 highlights the importance of continuous learning: "Give instruction to a wise man, and he will be yet wiser: teach a just man, and he will increase in learning." By being open to continuous learning and improvement, Christians can maintain their dedication to God and grow in their faith.

Both wrestlers and Christians must also practice patience and perseverance as part of their dedication. Wrestlers understand that success does not come overnight and that it takes time, effort, and persistence to achieve their goals. They learn to be patient with themselves, embracing the process of growth and improvement. Similarly, Christians must be patient and persevere in their faith journey, understanding that spiritual growth takes time and effort. They trust in God's timing and remain steadfast in their commitment to Him, even when faced with challenges and setbacks. Galatians 6:9

encourages believers to remain steadfast: "And let us not be weary in well doing: for in due season we shall reap, if we faint not." By practicing patience and perseverance, Christians can maintain their dedication to God and continue growing in their faith.

Both wrestlers and Christians must also cultivate a strong sense of purpose and identity. Wrestlers who have a clear understanding of their goals and values are better equipped to stay dedicated to their sport. They know why they are training, what they want to achieve, and what they stand for. This sense of purpose drives their dedication and keeps them focused on their goals. Similarly, Christians who have a strong sense of their identity in Christ and their purpose in God's plan are better equipped to stay dedicated to their faith. They understand that their ultimate goal is to glorify God and fulfill His purposes for their lives. Ephesians 2:10 reminds believers of their identity and purpose: "For

we are his workmanship, created in Christ Jesus unto good works, which God hath before ordained that we should walk in them." By understanding their purpose and identity, Christians can find the motivation and strength to stay dedicated to God and live according to His will.

In conclusion, focusing on the goal is essential in both wrestling and the Christian life, requiring unwavering determination, clear vision, and a steadfast commitment to achieving one's objectives. Wrestlers exhibit dedication to their sport by adhering to rigorous training schedules, maintaining strict diets, and constantly working to improve their techniques and physical conditioning. Similarly, Christians show dedication to their faith by committing their hearts and lives to following Jesus and living according to God's Word. Philippians 3:14 emphasizes the importance of this commitment: "I press toward the mark for the prize of the high calling of God in Christ Jesus." By demonstrating perseverance, discipline, setting clear goals, making sacrifices, staying motivated, embracing continuous learning, practicing patience, and cultivating a strong sense of purpose, both wrestlers and Christians can maintain their dedication and achieve success in their respective journeys. By staying committed to their values and relying on their respective sources of strength, individuals in both contexts can honor their commitments, uphold their integrity, and ultimately bring glory to God.

Chapter 18 Overcoming Fear

Overcoming fear is a significant aspect of both wrestling and the Christian life, requiring individuals to confront their anxieties, develop courage, and rely on their training and faith to persevere. In wrestling, athletes often face the fear of losing or getting injured. This fear can be daunting and may affect their performance if not managed properly. Wrestlers must learn to overcome these fears through rigorous training, mental preparation, and a strong support system. They engage in physical conditioning and practice techniques repeatedly to build confidence in their abilities. By preparing thoroughly, wrestlers can trust in their skills and reduce the fear of losing. Coaches play a crucial role in helping wrestlers overcome fear by offering encouragement, strategies for staying focused, and mental exercises to boost confidence. Visualization techniques, where wrestlers imagine themselves succeeding, can also help reduce anxiety and build a positive mindset. The experience of stepping onto the mat, facing opponents, and learning from both victories and defeats helps wrestlers develop resilience and the ability to push through fear. This process of confronting and overcoming fear not only enhances their performance in the sport but also builds character and mental toughness that benefits them in all areas of life.

Similarly, Christians are called to overcome fear through faith, relying on God's promises and presence to navigate life's challenges. Fear can manifest in various forms, such as fear of the unknown, fear of failure, or fear of difficult circumstances. Isaiah 41:10 provides a powerful assurance for believers: "Fear thou not; for I am with thee: be not dismayed; for I am thy God: I will strengthen thee; yea, I will help thee; yea, I will uphold thee with the right hand of my righteousness." This verse encourages Christians to trust in God's strength and support, knowing that He is always with them. By placing their faith in God, believers can find the courage to face their fears and overcome them.

Regular prayer, reading the Bible, and participating in worship help Christians stay connected to God and draw strength from His promises. These spiritual practices provide comfort, guidance, and reassurance, helping believers navigate their fears with confidence.

Both wrestlers and Christians benefit from a strong support system to help them overcome fear. Wrestlers rely on coaches, teammates, and family members for encouragement and motivation. This support network provides a sense of security and helps wrestlers stay focused on their goals. Similarly, Christians find strength in their faith community, including pastors, mentors, and fellow believers. This community offers prayer, support, and accountability, helping individuals face their fears and grow in their faith. Hebrews 10:24-25 emphasizes the importance of mutual support: "And let us consider one another to provoke unto love and to good works: Not forsaking the assembling of ourselves together, as the manner of some is; but exhorting one another: and so much the more, as ye see the day approaching." By being part of a supportive community, both wrestlers and Christians can draw on the collective strength and encouragement of others to overcome fear.

Both wrestlers and Christians must also develop mental and spiritual resilience to face their fears. Wrestlers build mental resilience through consistent training, learning to stay calm under pressure, and focusing on their goals. They practice techniques to manage anxiety, such as deep breathing, visualization, and positive self-talk. These strategies help them stay composed and confident during competitions. Similarly, Christians develop spiritual resilience by trusting in God's plan and relying on His strength. They learn to surrender their fears to God and find peace in His presence. Philippians 4:6-7 offers guidance for managing anxiety: "Be careful for nothing; but in every thing by prayer and supplication with thanksgiving let your requests be made known unto God. And the peace of God, which passeth all understanding, shall keep your hearts and minds through Christ Jesus."

By maintaining a strong relationship with God, believers can find the peace and strength needed to overcome their fears.

Both wrestlers and Christians must also embrace the process of growth and learning from their experiences. Wrestlers understand that facing their fears and stepping onto the mat, despite the possibility of losing or getting injured, is essential for improvement. Each match, regardless of the outcome, provides valuable lessons that help them grow as athletes. Similarly, Christians recognize that overcoming fear is part of their spiritual journey. They learn to trust in God's timing and His ability to work through difficult situations. Romans 5:3-4 speaks to this process: "And not only so, but we glory in tribulations also: knowing that tribulation worketh patience; And patience, experience; and experience, hope." By embracing their experiences and trusting in God's plan, believers can grow stronger in their faith and develop the resilience needed to face future challenges.

Both wrestlers and Christians must also practice patience and perseverance in overcoming fear. Wrestlers understand that building confidence and reducing fear takes time and consistent effort. They learn to be patient with themselves, recognizing that progress may be slow but is still meaningful. They celebrate small victories and improvements, knowing that these incremental gains contribute to their overall success. Similarly, Christians must be patient and persevere in their faith journey, understanding that overcoming fear is a process that requires time and trust in God. They rely on God's promises and remain steadfast in their commitment to Him, even when faced with difficult circumstances. Galatians 6:9 encourages believers to remain steadfast: "And let us not be weary in well doing: for in due season we shall reap, if we faint not." By practicing patience and perseverance, Christians can maintain their faith and continue growing in their relationship with God.

Both wrestlers and Christians must also develop a strong sense of purpose and identity to overcome fear. Wrestlers who have a clear understanding of their goals and values are better equipped to face their fears and stay dedicated to their sport. They know why they are training, what they want to achieve, and what they stand for. This sense of purpose drives their dedication and helps them push through fear. Similarly, Christians who have a strong sense of their identity in Christ and their purpose in God's plan are better equipped to overcome fear. They understand that their ultimate goal is to glorify God and fulfill His purposes for their lives. Ephesians 2:10 reminds believers of their identity and purpose: "For we are his workmanship, created in Christ Jesus unto good works, which God hath before ordained that we should walk in them." By understanding their purpose and identity, Christians can find the motivation and strength to overcome fear and live according to God's will.

In conclusion, overcoming fear is a significant aspect of both wrestling and the Christian life, requiring individuals to confront their anxieties, develop courage, and rely on their training and faith to persevere. Wrestlers face the fear of losing or getting injured and must learn to overcome these fears through rigorous training, mental preparation, and a strong support system. Similarly, Christians are called to overcome fear through faith, relying on God's promises and presence to navigate life's challenges. Isaiah 41:10 provides a powerful assurance for believers: "Fear thou not; for I am with thee: be not dismayed; for I am thy God: I will strengthen thee; yea, I will help thee; yea, I will uphold thee with the right hand of my righteousness." By developing mental and spiritual resilience, practicing patience and perseverance, and understanding their purpose and identity, both wrestlers and Christians can overcome fear and achieve their goals. By staying committed to their values and relying on their respective sources of strength, individuals in both contexts can honor their commitments, uphold their integrity, and ultimately bring glory to God.

Chapter 19 Integrity

Integrity is an essential quality in both wrestling and the Christian life, requiring individuals to adhere to moral principles, act honestly, and maintain a commitment to ethical behavior in all circumstances. In wrestling, athletes must compete with integrity, upholding the values of sportsmanship, fairness, and respect. This means following the rules of the sport, treating opponents with respect, and striving to win through hard work and skill rather than through cheating or dishonesty. Wrestlers learn that true success is not just about winning matches but about how they conduct themselves both on and off the mat. Coaches play a crucial role in instilling these values, teaching wrestlers the importance of integrity and holding them accountable for their actions. Competing with integrity builds trust and respect among teammates, opponents, and the broader wrestling community. It also builds character, teaching wrestlers valuable life lessons about honesty, perseverance, and ethical conduct that extend beyond the sport.

Similarly, Christians are called to live with integrity, adhering to God's moral standards and reflecting His character in their daily lives. Proverbs 10:9 emphasizes the importance of integrity: "He that walketh uprightly walketh surely: but he that perverteth his ways shall be known." This verse underscores that living with integrity provides a firm foundation and a sense of security, while dishonesty and unethical behavior eventually lead to exposure and consequences. For Christians, living with integrity means being honest, trustworthy, and consistent in their actions and decisions. It involves aligning one's behavior with biblical principles, being truthful in all dealings, and demonstrating integrity in relationships, work, and personal conduct. By living with integrity, Christians bear witness to their faith and honor God, who calls His people to be holy and righteous.

Both wrestlers and Christians benefit from a strong sense of accountability in maintaining their integrity. In wrestling, athletes rely on coaches, teammates, and mentors to hold them accountable for their actions and ensure they compete fairly. This accountability helps wrestlers stay focused on their values and resist the temptation to cheat or cut corners. It also fosters a culture of mutual respect and ethical behavior within the team. Similarly, Christians benefit from the accountability provided by their faith community. Fellow believers, pastors, and spiritual mentors can offer encouragement, guidance, and support, helping individuals stay committed to their moral principles and grow in their faith. Hebrews 10:24-25 highlights the importance of mutual encouragement and accountability: "And let us consider one another to provoke unto love and to good works: Not forsaking the assembling of ourselves together, as the manner of some is; but exhorting one another: and so much the more, as ye see the day approaching." By being part of a supportive community, Christians can draw on the strength and encouragement of others to maintain their integrity.

Both wrestlers and Christians must also practice self-discipline to uphold their integrity. Wrestlers follow strict training regimens, adhere to dietary guidelines, and consistently work on improving their skills. This discipline helps them stay focused on their goals and maintain their commitment to ethical behavior, even when faced with challenges or temptations. Similarly, Christians practice spiritual disciplines such as prayer, Bible study, worship, and fellowship to nurture their relationship with God and strengthen their commitment to living with integrity. These practices help believers stay connected to God, draw on His strength, and remain steadfast in their moral convictions. By consistently engaging in these disciplines, Christians build a strong foundation of faith that supports them in maintaining their integrity in all aspects of life.

Both wrestlers and Christians must also embrace the importance of honesty in their pursuit of integrity. In wrestling, athletes must be honest with themselves about their strengths and weaknesses, seeking to improve through hard work and dedication rather than resorting to dishonest means. This honesty extends to their interactions with coaches, teammates, and opponents, fostering a culture of trust and respect. Similarly, Christians are called to be honest in all their dealings, recognizing that God values truth and transparency. Proverbs 12:22 underscores the value of honesty: "Lying lips are abomination to the Lord: but they that deal truly are his delight." By being honest in their words and actions, Christians reflect God's character and build trust with others.

Both wrestlers and Christians must also recognize the long-term benefits of living with integrity. For wrestlers, competing with integrity builds a reputation of trustworthiness and respect that can open doors for future opportunities, whether in the sport or in other areas of life. It also fosters a sense of personal satisfaction and pride in knowing that they have conducted themselves honorably. Similarly, Christians who live with integrity experience the long-term benefits of a clear conscience, strong relationships, and the peace that comes from knowing they are honoring God. Proverbs 11:3 highlights the guiding power of integrity: "The integrity of the upright shall guide them: but the perverseness of transgressors shall destroy them." By living with integrity, Christians can navigate life's challenges with confidence, knowing that they are following God's path.

Both wrestlers and Christians must also be prepared to face challenges and temptations that test their integrity. Wrestlers may encounter opportunities to cheat, take shortcuts, or engage in unsportsmanlike behavior, especially under pressure to win. Maintaining integrity requires a strong commitment to ethical principles and the courage to do what is right, even when it is difficult. Similarly, Christians face various temptations that can compromise their integrity, such as dishonesty, greed, or compromising their values for personal gain. Overcoming these challenges requires a deep reliance on God's strength and guidance. 1 Corinthians 10:13 offers encouragement for facing temptation: "There hath no temptation taken you but such as is common to man: but God is faithful, who will not suffer you to be tempted above that ye are able; but will with the temptation also make a way to escape, that ye may be able to bear it." By trusting in God's faithfulness, Christians can find the strength to resist temptation and uphold their integrity.

Both wrestlers and Christians must also understand the impact of their integrity on others. Wrestlers who compete with integrity set a positive example for their teammates, opponents, and the broader community, demonstrating that success can be achieved through honest and ethical means. Their actions can inspire others to uphold similar values and contribute to a culture of fairness and respect in the sport. Similarly, Christians who live with integrity reflect God's character to those around them, serving as a witness to the transformative power of faith. Their consistent commitment to ethical behavior can influence others to seek God and embrace His principles. Matthew 5:16 encourages believers to let their light shine: "Let your light so shine before men, that they may see your good works, and glorify your Father which is in heaven." By living with integrity, Christians can positively impact their communities and bring glory to God.

Both wrestlers and Christians must also be willing to stand up for what is right, even when it is unpopular or challenging. Wrestlers may face situations where they need to speak out against unethical behavior, advocate for fair play, or support teammates who are being treated unfairly. This courage to stand up for what is right reinforces their commitment to integrity and sets a strong example for others. Similarly, Christians are called to stand up for righteousness, defend the oppressed, and speak out against injustice. This may require courage and a willingness to face criticism or opposition, but it is a vital aspect of living with integrity. Micah 6:8 outlines God's requirement for His people: "He hath shewed thee, O man, what is good; and what doth the Lord require of thee, but to do justly, and to love mercy, and to walk humbly with thy God?" By standing up for what is right, Christians demonstrate their commitment to God's principles and make a positive impact on the world.

Both wrestlers and Christians must also cultivate humility as part of their commitment to integrity. Wrestlers who are humble recognize that their success is the result of hard work, the support of others, and the grace of opportunities. They treat their opponents with respect, acknowledge their own mistakes, and remain open to learning and improvement. Similarly, Christians are called to live humbly, recognizing their dependence on God and the importance of serving others. Humility helps believers maintain a proper perspective, avoid pride, and remain focused on their commitment to integrity. Philippians 2:3-4 encourages humility: "Let nothing be done through strife or vainglory; but in lowliness of mind let each esteem other better than themselves. Look not every man on his own things, but every man also on the things of others." By cultivating humility, Christians can live with integrity and reflect God's love to those around them.

In conclusion, integrity is an essential quality in both wrestling and the Christian life, requiring individuals to adhere to moral principles, act honestly, and maintain a commitment to ethical behavior in all circumstances. Wrestlers must compete with integrity, upholding the values of sportsmanship, fairness, and respect. Similarly, Christians are called to live with integrity, adhering to God's moral standards and reflecting His character in their daily lives. Proverbs 10:9 emphasizes the importance of integrity: "He that walketh uprightly walketh surely: but he that perverteth his ways shall be known." By practicing self-discipline, embracing honesty, understanding the long-term benefits, facing challenges, considering their impact on others, standing up for what is right, and cultivating humility, both wrestlers and Christians can maintain their integrity and achieve success in their respective journeys. By staying committed to their values and relying on their respective sources of strength, individuals in both contexts can honor their commitments, uphold their integrity, and ultimately bring glory to God.

Chapter 20 Learning from Defeat

Learning from defeat is a crucial aspect of both wrestling and the Christian life, teaching individuals resilience, humility, and the importance of growth through challenges. In wrestling, athletes often face losses that test their character and determination. These defeats can be difficult to handle, but they provide valuable lessons that help wrestlers improve. When a wrestler loses a match, it is an opportunity to analyze what went wrong and identify areas for improvement. Coaches play a significant role in this process, reviewing matches with their athletes, pointing out mistakes, and suggesting strategies for improvement. Wrestlers learn to approach their defeats with a mindset of growth rather than discouragement. They understand that every loss is a stepping stone to becoming a better athlete. This perspective helps them to stay motivated, work harder, and persist through the tough times. Wrestlers who learn from their defeats become more skilled, strategic, and mentally tough. They develop a deeper understanding of the sport, recognize their weaknesses, and transform them into strengths. This process not only improves their performance on the mat but also builds character and resilience that benefit them in all areas of life.

Similarly, Christians learn from their failures, understanding that setbacks and mistakes are part of the journey of faith. Romans 8:28 offers a powerful reminder of God's purpose in every situation: "And we know that all things work together for good to them that love God, to them who are the called according to his purpose." This verse assures believers that even their failures can be used by God for their good and His glory. When Christians face failures, whether in their personal lives, relationships, or spiritual walk, they are encouraged to see these moments as opportunities for growth. Instead of being paralyzed by guilt or disappointment, they are called to seek God's guidance, learn from their mistakes, and trust in His redemptive power. Through prayer, reflection, and studying the Bible, Christians can gain insight into their failures, understand what went wrong, and discern how to move forward. This process of learning from failure helps believers grow in their faith, develop greater humility, and deepen their reliance on God's grace and strength.

Both wrestlers and Christians benefit from the support and encouragement of others as they learn from their defeats and failures. Wrestlers rely on their coaches, teammates, and family members to help them process their losses, stay motivated, and continue striving for improvement. This support network provides a sense of community and helps wrestlers maintain a positive outlook, even in the face of setbacks. Similarly, Christians find strength in their faith community, which offers prayer, encouragement, and accountability. Fellow believers, pastors, and spiritual mentors can provide guidance and support, helping individuals navigate their failures and grow in their faith. Hebrews 10:24-25 emphasizes the importance of mutual support: "And let us consider one another to provoke unto love and to good works: Not forsaking the assembling of ourselves together, as the manner of some is; but exhorting one another: and so much the more, as ye see the day approaching." By being part of a supportive community, both wrestlers and Christians can draw on the collective strength and encouragement of others to overcome their defeats and failures.

Both wrestlers and Christians must also develop a mindset of perseverance and resilience in the face of defeat. Wrestlers learn that losing a match does not define their worth or potential. Instead, it is a temporary setback that can be overcome with hard work and determination. They learn to keep pushing forward, even when progress seems slow or obstacles seem insurmountable. This resilience helps them stay committed to their goals and continue improving. Similarly, Christians are called to persevere in their faith, trusting that God is working in their lives even through their failures. James 1:2-4 encourages believers to view trials as opportunities for growth: "My brethren, count it all joy when ye fall into divers temptations; Knowing this, that the trying of your faith worketh patience. But let patience have her perfect work, that ye may be perfect and entire, wanting nothing." By embracing a mindset of perseverance, Christians can overcome their failures and grow stronger in their relationship with God.

Both wrestlers and Christians must also practice humility in learning from their defeats and failures. Wrestlers who approach their losses with humility are willing to acknowledge their mistakes and seek feedback from their coaches and teammates. This humility allows them to learn and grow, rather than being held back by pride or denial. They recognize that improvement requires an honest assessment of their performance and a willingness to make changes. Similarly, Christians are called to approach their failures with humility, acknowledging their need for God's grace and guidance. 1 Peter 5:6 encourages believers to humble themselves before God: "Humble yourselves therefore under the mighty hand of God, that he may exalt you in due time." By practicing humility, Christians can learn from their failures and experience God's transformative power in their lives.

Both wrestlers and Christians must also be willing to take risks and step out of their comfort zones, knowing that failure is a possibility but also a valuable learning opportunity. Wrestlers understand that competing at a high level involves taking risks, trying new techniques, and pushing their limits. They learn that failure is part of the process of growth and improvement. This willingness to take risks helps them become more skilled and confident athletes. Similarly, Christians are called to step out in faith, take risks for God's kingdom, and trust that He will use their efforts for His purposes. This may involve sharing their faith, serving others, or pursuing a calling that stretches their abilities. By embracing risks and learning from the outcomes, Christians can grow in their faith and witness God's faithfulness.

Proverbs 3:5-6 encourages believers to trust in God's guidance: "Trust in the Lord with all thine heart; and lean not unto thine own understanding. In all thy ways acknowledge him, and he shall direct thy paths." By taking risks and trusting in God, Christians can learn from their failures and grow in their relationship with Him.

Both wrestlers and Christians must also recognize the importance of reflection and analysis in learning from their defeats and failures. Wrestlers review their matches, analyze their performance, and identify areas for improvement. This reflection helps them understand what went wrong and how to correct it. They use this analysis to develop new strategies and techniques for future competitions. Similarly, Christians are encouraged to reflect on their failures, seek God's wisdom, and learn from their experiences. Through prayer, Bible study, and seeking counsel from trusted mentors, believers can gain insight into their mistakes and discern how to move forward. Psalm 139:23-24 illustrates the importance of self-examination: "Search me, O God, and know my heart: try me, and know my thoughts: And see if there be any wicked way in me, and lead me in the way everlasting." By reflecting on their failures and seeking God's guidance, Christians can learn and grow in their faith.

Both wrestlers and Christians must also cultivate a positive and hopeful attitude in the face of defeat and failure. Wrestlers learn that a positive mindset is crucial for overcoming setbacks and staying motivated. They focus on their progress, celebrate small victories, and maintain hope for future success. This positive attitude helps them stay resilient and continue striving for improvement. Similarly, Christians are called to maintain a hopeful outlook, trusting in God's promises and His ability to work all things for good. Romans 8:28 provides assurance of God's redemptive power: "And we know that all things work together for good to them that love God, to them who are the called according to his purpose." By maintaining hope and trusting in

God's faithfulness, Christians can overcome their failures and grow stronger in their faith.

Both wrestlers and Christians must also understand the role of grace and forgiveness in learning from their defeats and failures. Wrestlers who experience defeat must learn to forgive themselves, let go of past mistakes, and move forward with a renewed focus. This process of self-forgiveness allows them to continue growing and improving without being weighed down by regret. Similarly, Christians are called to embrace God's grace and forgiveness, recognizing that their failures do not define them. God's grace provides the opportunity for a fresh start and the strength to overcome past mistakes. Ephesians 1:7 highlights the redemptive power of God's grace: "In whom we have redemption through his blood, the forgiveness of sins, according to the riches of his grace." By embracing grace and forgiveness, Christians can learn from their failures and continue growing in their relationship with God.

Both wrestlers and Christians must also commit to continuous learning and improvement. Wrestlers understand that growth is an ongoing process that requires dedication, practice, and a willingness to learn from every experience. They seek feedback, refine their techniques, and consistently work towards becoming better athletes. Similarly, Christians are called to continually grow in their faith, seeking God's guidance and striving to live according to His will. This commitment to continuous learning involves regular prayer, Bible study, and fellowship with other believers. 2 Peter 3:18 encourages believers to grow in their faith: "But grow in grace, and in the knowledge of our Lord and Saviour Jesus Christ. To him be glory both now and for ever. Amen." By committing to continuous learning and improvement, Christians can grow in their faith and better reflect God's love and character.

In conclusion, learning from defeat is a crucial aspect of both wrestling and the Christian life, teaching individuals resilience, humility, and the importance of growth through challenges. Wrestlers often face losses that test their character and determination, but they learn to approach these defeats with a mindset of growth, analyzing their performance and making improvements. Similarly, Christians learn from their failures, understanding that setbacks and mistakes are part of the journey of faith. Romans 8:28 offers a powerful reminder of God's purpose in every situation: "And we know that all things work together for good to them that love God, to them who are the called according to his purpose." By embracing the support of others, practicing perseverance and humility, taking risks, reflecting on experiences, maintaining a positive attitude, embracing grace and forgiveness, and committing to continuous learning, both wrestlers and Christians can learn from their defeats and failures and grow stronger in their respective journeys. By staying committed to their values and relying on their respective sources of strength, individuals in both contexts can overcome their challenges, uphold their integrity, and ultimately bring glory to God.

Chapter 21 Courage

Courage is a vital quality in both wrestling and the Christian life, requiring individuals to face their fears, take risks, and stand firm in challenging situations. In wrestling, athletes demonstrate courage every time they step into the ring, confronting not only their opponents but also their own fears and doubts. Wrestling is an intense and physically demanding sport that pushes athletes to their limits. Wrestlers must have the courage to endure physical pain, confront stronger or more skilled opponents, and push through the fear of failure or injury. This courage is developed through rigorous training, mental preparation, and the support of coaches and teammates. Coaches play a crucial role in fostering courage, encouraging wrestlers to take risks, believe in their abilities, and remain focused under pressure. Wrestlers learn to manage their fears, stay calm and composed, and face each match with determination and confidence. This courage on the mat translates into other areas of life, helping wrestlers build resilience, confidence, and the ability to tackle challenges head-on.

Similarly, Christians are called to show courage in their faith, standing firm in their beliefs and trusting in God's promises, even in the face of adversity. Joshua 1:9 provides a powerful reminder of God's command and assurance: "Have not I commanded thee? Be strong and of a good courage; be not afraid, neither be thou dismayed: for the LORD thy God is with thee whithersoever thou goest." This verse encourages believers to be strong and courageous, knowing that God is always with them. Courage in the Christian life involves standing up for one's faith, sharing the gospel, and living according to God's principles, even when it is difficult or unpopular. Christians may face persecution, ridicule, or pressure to conform to worldly standards, but they are called to remain steadfast and trust in God's presence and strength. This courage is nurtured through prayer, reading the Bible, and fellowship with other believers. By drawing close to God and relying on His promises, Christians can find the strength and courage to live out their faith boldly.

Both wrestlers and Christians benefit from a strong support system to help them develop and maintain their courage. Wrestlers rely on coaches, teammates, and family members for encouragement and motivation. This support network provides a sense of security and helps wrestlers stay focused on their goals. Similarly, Christians find strength in their faith community, which offers prayer, encouragement, and accountability. Fellow believers, pastors, and spiritual mentors can provide guidance and support, helping individuals navigate their fears and grow in their faith. Hebrews 10:24-25 emphasizes the importance of mutual support: "And let us consider one another to provoke unto love and to good works: Not forsaking the assembling of ourselves together, as the manner of some is; but exhorting one another: and so much the more, as ye see the day approaching." By being part of a supportive community, both wrestlers and Christians can draw on the collective strength and encouragement of others to face their challenges with courage.

Both wrestlers and Christians must also develop mental and spiritual resilience to face their fears and demonstrate courage. Wrestlers build mental resilience through consistent training, learning to stay calm under pressure, and focusing on their goals. They practice techniques to manage anxiety, such as deep breathing, visualization, and positive self-talk. These strategies help them stay composed and confident during competitions. Similarly, Christians develop spiritual resilience by trusting in God's plan and relying on His strength. They learn to surrender their fears to God and find peace in His presence. Philippians 4:6-7 offers guidance for managing anxiety: "Be careful for nothing; but in every thing by prayer and supplication with thanksgiving let your requests be made known unto God. And the peace of God, which passeth all understanding, shall keep your hearts and minds through Christ Jesus." By maintaining a strong relationship with God, believers can find the peace and strength needed to overcome their fears and live courageously.

Both wrestlers and Christians must also embrace the process of growth and learning from their experiences. Wrestlers understand that facing their fears and stepping onto the mat, despite the possibility of losing or getting injured, is essential for improvement. Each match, regardless of the outcome, provides valuable lessons that help them grow as athletes. Similarly, Christians recognize that overcoming fear is part of their spiritual journey. They learn to trust in God's timing and His ability to work through difficult situations. Romans 5:3-4 speaks to this process: "And not only so, but we glory in tribulations also: knowing that tribulation worketh patience; And patience, experience; and experience, hope." By embracing their experiences and trusting in God's plan, believers can grow stronger in their faith and develop the resilience needed to face future challenges with courage.

Both wrestlers and Christians must also practice patience and perseverance in demonstrating courage. Wrestlers understand that building confidence and reducing fear takes time and consistent effort. They learn to be patient with themselves, recognizing that progress may be slow but is still meaningful. They celebrate small victories and improvements, knowing that these incremental gains contribute to their overall success. Similarly, Christians must be patient and persevere in their faith journey, understanding that developing courage is a process that requires time and trust in God. They rely on God's promises and remain steadfast in their commitment to Him, even when faced with difficult circumstances. Galatians 6:9 encourages believers to remain steadfast: "And let us not be weary in well doing: for in due season we shall reap, if we faint not." By practicing patience and perseverance, Christians can maintain their faith and continue growing in their relationship with God, demonstrating courage in all areas of life.

Both wrestlers and Christians must also develop a strong sense of purpose and identity to demonstrate courage. Wrestlers who have a clear understanding of their goals and values are better equipped to face their fears and stay dedicated to their sport. They know why they are training, what they want to achieve, and what they stand for. This sense of purpose drives their dedication and helps them push through fear. Similarly, Christians who have a strong sense of their identity in Christ and their purpose in God's plan are better equipped to overcome fear. They understand that their ultimate goal is to glorify God and fulfill His purposes for their lives. Ephesians 2:10 reminds believers of their identity and purpose: "For we are his workmanship, created in Christ Jesus unto good works, which God hath before ordained that we should walk in them." By understanding their purpose and identity, Christians can find the motivation and strength to overcome fear and live according to God's will.

Both wrestlers and Christians must also be willing to take risks and step out of their comfort zones, knowing that courage involves facing the unknown and trusting in their abilities and faith. Wrestlers understand that competing at a high level involves taking risks, trying new techniques, and pushing their limits. They learn that fear is a natural part of the process of growth and improvement. This willingness to take risks helps them become more skilled and confident athletes. Similarly, Christians are called to step out in faith, take risks for God's kingdom, and trust that He will use their efforts for His purposes. This may involve sharing their faith, serving others, or pursuing a calling that stretches their abilities. By embracing risks and learning from the outcomes, Christians can grow in their faith and witness God's faithfulness. Proverbs 3:5-6 encourages believers to trust in God's guidance: "Trust in the Lord with all thine heart; and lean not unto thine own understanding. In all thy ways acknowledge him, and he shall direct thy paths." By taking risks and trusting in God,

Christians can learn from their experiences and grow in their relationship with Him, demonstrating courage in all they do.

Both wrestlers and Christians must also cultivate a positive and hopeful attitude in the face of fear and challenges. Wrestlers learn that a positive mindset is crucial for overcoming setbacks and staying motivated. They focus on their progress, celebrate small victories, and maintain hope for future success. This positive attitude helps them stay resilient and continue striving for improvement. Similarly, Christians are called to maintain a hopeful outlook, trusting in God's promises and His ability to work all things for good. Romans 8:28 provides assurance of God's redemptive power: "And we know that all things work together for good to them that love God, to them who are the called according to his purpose." By maintaining hope and trusting in God's faithfulness, Christians can overcome their fears and grow stronger in their faith, demonstrating courage in their daily lives.

Both wrestlers and Christians must also understand the role of grace and forgiveness in demonstrating courage. Wrestlers who experience defeat or make mistakes must learn to forgive themselves, let go of past mistakes, and move forward with a renewed focus. This process of self forgiveness allows them to continue growing and improving without being weighed down by regret. Similarly, Christians are called to embrace God's grace and forgiveness, recognizing that their failures do not define them. God's grace provides the opportunity for a fresh start and the strength to overcome past mistakes. Ephesians 1:7 highlights the redemptive power of God's grace: "In whom we have redemption through his blood, the forgiveness of sins, according to the riches of his grace." By embracing grace and forgiveness, Christians can learn from their failures and continue growing in their relationship with God, demonstrating courage in all they do.

Both wrestlers and Christians must also commit to continuous learning and improvement. Wrestlers understand that growth is an ongoing process that requires dedication, practice, and a willingness to learn from every experience. They seek feedback, refine their techniques, and consistently work towards becoming better athletes. Similarly, Christians are called to continually grow in their faith, seeking God's guidance and striving to live according to His will. This commitment to continuous learning involves regular prayer, Bible study, and fellowship with other believers. 2 Peter 3:18 encourages believers to grow in their faith: "But grow in grace, and in the knowledge of our Lord and Saviour Jesus Christ. To him be glory both now and for ever. Amen." By committing to continuous learning and improvement, Christians

can grow in their faith and better reflect God's love and character, demonstrating courage in their spiritual journey.

In conclusion, courage is a vital quality in both wrestling and the Christian life, requiring individuals to face their fears, take risks, and stand firm in challenging situations. Wrestlers demonstrate courage every time they step into the ring, confronting their opponents and their own fears and doubts. Similarly, Christians are called to show courage in their faith, standing firm in their beliefs and trusting in God's promises, even in the face of adversity. Joshua 1:9 provides a powerful reminder of God's command and assurance: "Have not I commanded thee? Be strong and of a good courage; be not afraid, neither be thou dismayed: for the LORD thy God is with thee whithersoever thou goest." By developing mental and spiritual resilience, embracing growth, practicing patience and perseverance, understanding their purpose and identity, taking risks, maintaining a positive attitude, embracing grace and forgiveness, and committing to continuous learning, both wrestlers and Christians can demonstrate courage and achieve success in their respective journeys. By staying committed to their values and relying on their respective sources of strength, individuals in both contexts can honor their commitments, uphold their integrity, and ultimately bring glory to God.

Chapter 22 Victory Celebration

Victory celebration is a significant and joyful experience in both wrestling and the Christian life, symbolizing the culmination of hard work, perseverance, and overcoming challenges. In wrestling, athletes celebrate their victories as a testament to their dedication, skill, and resilience. Each win represents hours of intense training, strategic preparation, and mental fortitude. When wrestlers triumph in a match, it is not only a personal achievement but also a shared joy with coaches, teammates, and supporters who have been part of their journey. The victory celebration often involves cheers, high-fives, hugs, and sometimes even lifting the victor high in the air. These moments of triumph are cherished and remembered, providing motivation and encouragement for future challenges. They reinforce the value of hard work, discipline, and perseverance, and they strengthen the bonds within the team, fostering a sense of camaraderie and collective pride. Victory celebrations in wrestling are not just about the glory of winning but also about appreciating the journey, recognizing the support system, and looking forward to continued success.

Similarly, in the Christian life, believers anticipate the ultimate victory celebration, which is eternal life with Christ. This celebration signifies the fulfillment of God's promises and the end of all earthly suffering and trials. Revelation 21:4 paints a beautiful picture of this eternal joy: "And God shall wipe away all tears from their eyes; and there shall be no more death, neither sorrow, nor crying, neither shall there be any more pain: for the former things are passed away." This verse assures Christians that a time is coming when all the pain, sorrow, and struggles of this world will be replaced with everlasting peace, joy, and communion with God. The victory celebration in the Christian life is not just a future event but also influences how believers live in the present. It gives them hope, purpose, and strength to endure life's difficulties, knowing that their faith and perseverance will be rewarded. This hope of eternal life encourages Christians to remain steadfast in their faith, serve others, and live according to God's will, as they look forward to the ultimate celebration with Christ.

Both wrestlers and Christians understand that victory celebrations are a culmination of a journey marked by hard work, dedication, and overcoming obstacles. Wrestlers train rigorously, pushing their physical and mental limits to prepare for competitions. They learn to cope with setbacks, injuries, and defeats, using each experience as a lesson to improve and grow stronger. When they finally achieve victory, the celebration is a recognition of all the effort and sacrifices they have made. Similarly, Christians face various trials and temptations in their spiritual journey. They strive to live according to God's commandments, grow in their faith, and overcome the challenges that test their commitment. The promise of eternal life with Christ serves as a beacon of hope, encouraging them to persevere and remain faithful. The victory celebration in heaven will be a time of rejoicing and gratitude for God's grace and faithfulness throughout their lives.

Both wrestlers and Christians also recognize the importance of sharing their victories with others. In wrestling, a victory is often celebrated with coaches, teammates, family, and friends who have supported the athlete along the way. This shared celebration strengthens relationships and fosters a sense of community. It acknowledges that success is not achieved alone but through the collective effort and support of many. Similarly, Christians look forward to celebrating eternal life with fellow believers. The victory celebration in heaven will be a communal event, where all who have trusted in Christ will join together in worship and praise. This shared joy reflects the unity and fellowship of the body of Christ, where each member's journey and triumph contribute to the collective celebration.

Both wrestlers and Christians must also remember to celebrate victories with humility and gratitude. Wrestlers, while enjoying their success, should acknowledge the efforts of their opponents, the guidance of their coaches, and the support of their teammates. This humility keeps them grounded and focused on continuous improvement. They understand that each victory is a step in their ongoing journey and that there are always new challenges to face. Similarly, Christians are called to celebrate their spiritual victories with humility and gratitude to God. They recognize that their salvation and eternal life are not earned by their own efforts but are gifts of God's grace. Ephesians 2:8-9 reminds believers of this truth: "For by grace are ye saved through faith; and that not of yourselves: it is the gift of God: Not of works, lest any man should boast." This humility fosters a spirit of thankfulness and worship, acknowledging God's sovereignty and goodness.

Both wrestlers and Christians can draw inspiration from their victory celebrations for future challenges. For wrestlers, celebrating a win provides a boost of confidence and motivation to continue training and striving for excellence. It reminds them of what they are capable of achieving and encourages them to set new goals. Each victory serves as a reminder that hard work and perseverance pay off. Similarly, for Christians, the hope of eternal life and the promise of a future victory celebration inspire them to live faithfully and purposefully. Knowing that their ultimate reward awaits them, they are encouraged to persevere in their faith, serve others, and share the gospel. 1 Corinthians 15:58 provides this encouragement: "Therefore, my beloved brethren, be ye stedfast, unmoveable, always abounding in the work of the Lord, forasmuch as ye know that your labour is not in vain in the Lord."

Both wrestlers and Christians understand that victories, whether on the mat or in the spiritual realm, are milestones in a larger journey. For wrestlers, each victory is part of their ongoing development as athletes. It marks progress and improvement but also signifies the need to continue working hard and facing new challenges. They celebrate their successes but remain focused on their long-term goals and aspirations. Similarly, Christians view their spiritual victories as part of their lifelong journey of faith. Each step of growth, each act of service, and each moment of perseverance is a part of their preparation for eternity with Christ. The ultimate victory celebration in heaven is the culmination of their earthly journey, where they will experience the fullness of God's presence and glory.

In conclusion, victory celebration is a significant and joyful experience in both wrestling and the Christian life, symbolizing the culmination of hard work, perseverance, and overcoming challenges. Wrestlers celebrate their victories as a testament to their dedication, skill, and resilience, sharing the joy with coaches, teammates, and supporters. Similarly, Christians anticipate the ultimate victory celebration of eternal life with Christ, a time when all earthly suffering will be replaced with everlasting joy and peace. Revelation 21:4 beautifully captures this promise: "And God shall wipe away all tears from their eyes; and there shall be no more death, neither sorrow, nor crying, neither shall there be any more pain: for the former things are passed away." Both wrestlers and Christians recognize the importance of sharing their victories with others, celebrating with humility and gratitude, and drawing inspiration for future challenges. By staying committed to their values and relying on their respective sources of strength, individuals in both contexts can honor their commitments, uphold their integrity, and ultimately bring glory to God through their celebrations of victory.

Conclusion

As we reach the end of "The Champion's Faith- Wrestling and Achieving Spiritual Victory," it's clear that the journey of faith is a lot like a wrestling match. We've learned that in life, just like in wrestling, there will be times when we feel pinned down by our struggles, but it's in these moments that our faith is truly tested and strengthened. Every challenge, every doubt, and every fear is an opportunity to grow stronger, to dig deep, and to rely on the faith that God has given us. The lessons from the wrestling mat—discipline, perseverance, and the willingness to keep going even when things get tough—are the same principles that can help us overcome the spiritual battles we face every day. We've seen how champions are made, not just through physical strength, but through the inner strength that comes from trusting in God and believing in His plan for our lives. Whether you're fighting against temptation, fear, or any other challenge, remember that victory isn't just about winning the match; it's about staying in the fight, never giving up, and relying on God to give you the strength you need. As you step out of the ring and back into the world, carry these lessons with you. Keep training your heart and mind in faith, stay strong in the face of adversity, and always remember that with God on your side, you are more than a conqueror. The true victory lies not just in overcoming the challenges but in the faith that grows and strengthens with each battle. So, keep wrestling, keep believing, and keep striving for that ultimate spiritual victory that is yours through Christ.

Don't miss out!

Visit the website below and you can sign up to receive emails whenever Joshua Rhoades publishes a new book. There's no charge and no obligation.

https://books2read.com/r/B-A-AJLBB-MQIYE

BOOKS 2 READ

Connecting independent readers to independent writers.

Did you love *The Champion's Faith - Wrestling and Achieving Spiritual Victory*? Then you should read *From Dugout to Devotion- Spiritual Lessons from Baseball*[1] by Joshua Rhoades!

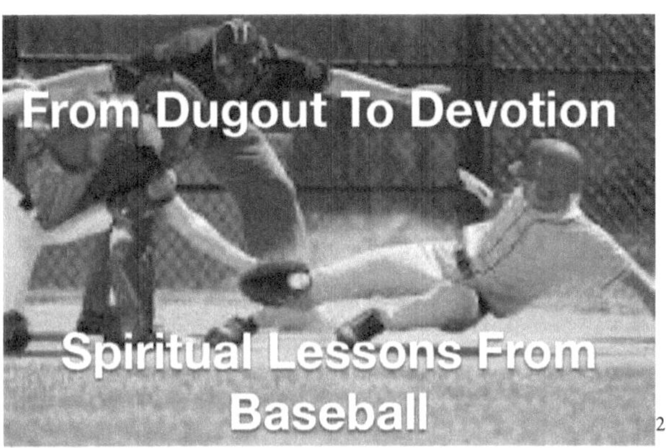

[2]

"From Dugout to Devotion: Spiritual Lessons from Baseball" invites you to step onto the diamond not just as a fan of the game, but as a seeker of deeper truths. Baseball is more than just a sport; it's a reflection of life itself, filled with moments of triumph, defeat, perseverance, and grace. As the bat cracks against the ball and the crowd holds its breath, there's more at play than just the game. Beneath the surface, baseball is rich with spiritual parallels that speak to the heart of our faith journey.

In every pitch, swing, and catch, there are lessons that echo the very principles of our Christian walk. The dugout, a place of preparation and strategy, mirrors our need for spiritual readiness and the importance of being grounded in God's Word. Just as players study their opponents and prepare for the game, we too must equip ourselves with spiritual wisdom and understanding to navigate the challenges we face in life. The devotion that drives a player to train, to push through

---

1. https://books2read.com/u/mdEJ0X

2. https://books2read.com/u/mdEJ0X

pain and fatigue, mirrors the perseverance we are called to have in our faith—a devotion to God that requires discipline, dedication, and trust.

This book takes you on a journey through the innings of life, drawing out spiritual insights from the game of baseball that can transform your walk with the Lord. It's about more than just the love of the game; it's about finding God's hand in every play, every challenge, and every victory. Whether you're standing in the batter's box, facing a curveball life has thrown your way, or running the bases, striving toward your goals, the lessons gleaned from baseball can guide you in your spiritual journey.

Through the pages of "From Dugout to Devotion," you'll discover how the discipline, teamwork, and perseverance required on the field are the same virtues needed in our spiritual lives. The patience of waiting for the right pitch, the courage to swing even when the outcome is uncertain, and the resilience to get back up after a strikeout all mirror the spiritual truths we encounter in our walk with Christ. Each chapter delves into these parallels, offering encouragement, wisdom, and practical applications to help you grow in your faith.

Whether you're a lifelong baseball fan or new to the sport, this book will open your eyes to the deeper spiritual lessons that can be found in the game. It will challenge you to see your faith in a new light, to draw strength from the timeless truths embedded in the game, and to apply these lessons to your own life. As you turn the pages, you'll be inspired to approach your faith with the same passion and dedication that drives a baseball player to strive for excellence. "From Dugout to Devotion" is more than just a book—it's a call to deepen your relationship with God through the timeless lessons found in America's favorite pastime. So, step up to the plate, and let the game begin.

* 9 7 9 8 2 2 7 6 4 9 5 6 0 *